MODELMAKING

W·W· Norton & Company · New York · London

MODELMAKING

A BASIC GUIDE

MARTHA SUTHERLAND

The text of this book is composed in Monotype
Walbaum with the display set in Graphite.

Composition by Ken Gross
Manufacturing by Courier Westford
Book design by Antonina Krass

**Library of Congress
Cataloging-in-Publication Data**

Sutherland, Martha, date.
Modelmaking : a basic guide / Martha Sutherland.
   p.   cm.
Includes index.
ISBN 0-393-73042-5
   1. Architectural models—Design and construction. I. Title.
NA2790.S87 1999
720'.22'8—dc21   99-25280
                      CIP

W. W. Norton & Company, Inc., 500 Fifth Avenue, New York, N.Y. 10110
www.wwnorton.com

W. W. Norton & Company Ltd., Castle House, 75/76 Wells Street, London W1T 3QT

0 9 8 7 6 5

CONTENTS

I . . . like models because they are so realistic. You can light them and photograph them and take them to bed and pretend that they are built.   —Emilio Ambasz

Credits

With the exception of several grids, all of the illustrations have been drawn freehand. The following list credits the sources for drawings labeled "in the spirit of" or identified in the text as based on an actual project.

INTRODUCTION

Architectural models may be small, large, simple, fancy, professional, or nonprofessional, but all fit into one of two genres: the study model or the presentation model. The study model's job is to clarify spaces. Made more quickly and with inexpensive materials, it is the architect and landscape architect's best tool for working out spatial problems, visualizing the interaction of volumes, and considering a building in relation to its site. It is a creative tool for the designer—a leap toward reality and away from the orthographic flatness of plan and elevation. Working out the geometries of space in three dimensions rather than in two can save you from serious misjudgments.

Creating viable spaces is the most cogent reason for building a study model, but such a model is also a place to play with modifications—the shape of a roof, for example. Half a dozen mockups could be popped into place for study and approval. Or, study models can be assembled in modules so that switching whole wings around is a simple matter.

Models are typically seen below eye level. Unfortunately, it is an artificial viewpoint, one from which a building is almost never seen. The designer must remember, particularly in the study-model stage, to hold up the model frequently, rotating it and observing it on a more

normal level. In the studio a cardboard carton can be used to prop up the model for consideration. If there is tack-board space, a piece of foamcore supported by a couple of triangular brackets will make a lightweight shelf.

The presentation model is the one shown to a jury or client. It may be simple or elaborate but is always meticulously constructed. Adopted for the pragmatic reason that all the world loves a miniature, the presentation model is a psychological ploy. Any skillfully crafted object inspires delight, but when the object is also small in scale it has the universal appeal of a puppy, a bird's egg, a dollhouse, or a jewel. Models sell ideas because they romanticize the object. The large made small endears itself effortlessly to the observer.

Many models are demountable. The roof and each floor can be removed to show the space within. Sections must be made to fit properly and be sturdy enough to stand up to the inevitable handling that will result when the word gets around that hey look, it comes apart!

Models obviously cannot be real buildings made small. They are symbols of real buildings and real sites, and they utilize a symbol vocabulary in which varying degrees of realism relate to varying scale. If the scale is small enough, say in a landscape architect's model of a large park, the buildings might simply be small, rectangular blocks of wood. More detail must be incorporated with larger models. At $\frac{1}{8}$" (1:100) scale window frames may not be necessary. At $\frac{1}{2}$" (1:20) scale they are probably essential. Color may or may not indicate a material: a white or gray model may represent painted wood or red brick. Your model should radiate the message you wish to convey. Banks, for example, usually project an aura of solidity, conservatism, and opulence. Quite certainly you would not create the same building for a summer house as for a city hall.

Choose your materials with your audience in mind. For classroom study, most models are made from plain illustration board. But a presentation to a city council, a hospital building committee, or a business magnate might be an opportunity to use materials in inventive ways—to delight or dazzle. A cautionary note: it is easy to be carried away with the fun of making an exciting model, but the material must not be allowed to outshine the design concept.

The classroom is not the model's only destination or reason for being. Private residence designs should be accompanied by a model, since few lay people are comfortable with architectural drawings. Commercial buildings need models, as do additions to existing buildings, restorations, and historic reconstructions. Models are made for commercial interiors—showcases, display walls, and stairways. And let's not forget the amateurs out there who just like to build miniatures of favorite places—cabins, treehouses, Indian kivas, dollhouses.

Modelmaking is intended as a primer for students in architecture, landscape architecture, interior design, and related fields. Others who want to make models—theater students, historians, and archeologists, for example—will also find it useful. The book considers the study model, but it is primarily intended to help a neophyte produce a creditable presentation model. Professional models, which employ the latest advances in high technology, computer imaging, and expensive equipment, are not discussed. Students will discover that in most moderate-sized offices, models are built in-house, and that being a good modelmaker is an advantage in the job market.

MODELMAKING

A BASIC GUIDE

1
Getting Started

The construction methods described in this book are basic. These methods are not only essential to getting started, but also vital as the complexity of your models increases. Beginning students need to learn the techniques shown, but it is patience, desire for excellence, and attention to detail that are the criteria for success. The modelmaker's skill determines the quality of the model—your second model will be demonstrably better than your first.

IMPORTANT EQUIPMENT

It is assumed that you have a drawing board with a T square or parallel bar. Don't forget to keep a paper towel or something nearby on which to wipe your hands. A clean model is a must. Your tools and materials may change depending upon the type of model you are making, but the following equipment is almost always necessary.

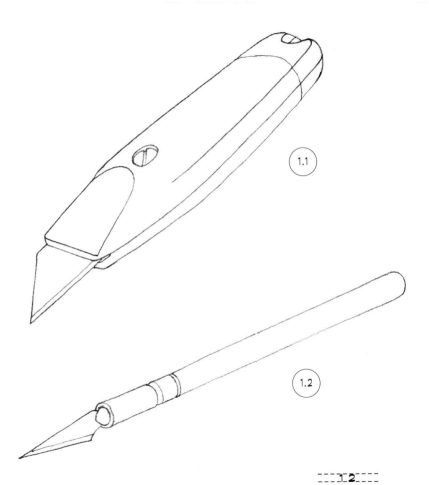

1.1

1.2

- Utility knife (figure 1.1). A heavy-duty knife with a comfortable, sturdy holder. Metal holders are better than plastic because they will last forever. This kind of knife has blades with two usable ends. Extra blades are stored in the handle.

- Craft knife (figure 1.2). A lightweight knife for cutting paper or lightweight materials. Ideal for cutting curves and small details. Caution: Throw away knife blades carefully—it's not nice to injure janitors. Stick the blade into a scrap of foamcore or fold drafting tape over the edge.

- Retractable blade knife (figure 1.3). These knives have scored blades that can be snapped off when they become dull. Be sure to find the kind that locks the blade in place. This knife has a heft and feel similar to the craft knife but is not as sturdy. Its advantage is its easily replaced blade.

- Hand-held board cutter and beveler (figure 1.4). A small, efficient mat cutter that can make clean, 45-degree-angle cuts. Using two blades at once, it can also cut strips or make

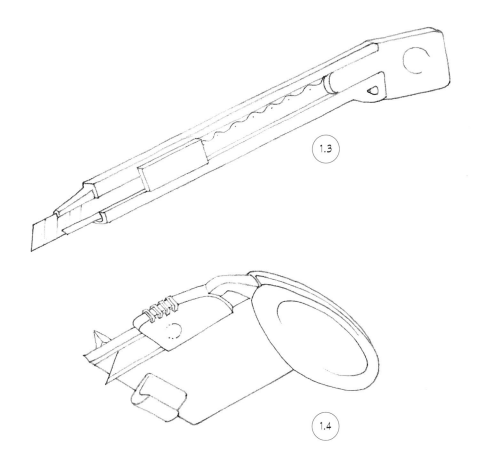

1.3

1.4

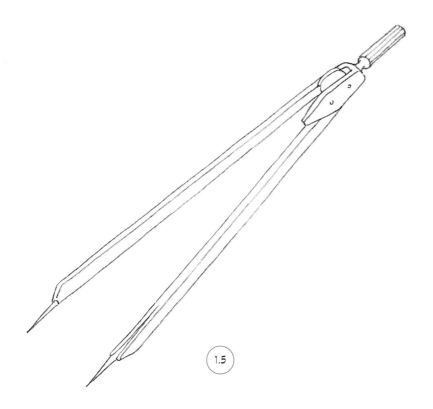

1.5

scores. (A score is a cut made partway through the material, allowing it to fold easily without breaking apart.)

- Dividers (figure 1.5). For hard-to-make measurements and units that are out of true.

- Metal ruler.

- Triangle. Both 30°-by-60° and 45°-by-45° triangles are used.

Other handy but not necessarily essential tools include: an architect's scale, engineer's scale, heavy needle (a candlewicking needle, number 20 tapestry needle, or cotton darner needle will do), circle template, protractor, and self-healing cutting board (this is expensive, but it saves surfaces, knife blades, and tempers). Also helpful (though costly) is a device called a model-scope. It is a pencil-sized, inverted periscope that can be inserted into the model and swiveled in any direction, providing a "walk through" view that is great fun as well as being informative. It is even possible to attach a camera to the model-scope and take photos of the model's interior.

MATERIALS

Beyond the basics—paper, illustration board, or some heavy card—the range of materials used in modelmaking is almost endless. Do not be afraid to experiment with different materials or to use them in inventive new ways. You will learn their properties and may make interesting discoveries. Take no chances with your model, though. If paint is involved, try it out first to check the color and to ensure that it doesn't adversely affect your material. Some sprays have been known to eat Styrofoam, for instance. If you are covering the board with paper, your glue job needs to be wrinkle-free, so experiment first. Below is a list of materials that you will need sooner or later if you continue modelmaking.

- Illustration board. A heavy cardboard with one side having a smooth, evenly textured surface suitable for drawing on. Available in hot or cold press, hot press being the smoothest.

- Poster (bristol) board. Thinner and cheaper than illustration board. Its surface is smooth and shiny on both sides.

- Chipboard (pulpboard). Inexpensive, usually gray, cardboard-type material with uniform sides. Available in several weights.

- Museum board. A heavy paper with a very soft surface.

- Foamcore (foamboard). A foam plastic filling sandwiched between two sheets of slick paper. Very lightweight.

- Canson paper. A toothy drawing paper available in a wide variety of colors.

- Balsa wood and basswood. Soft, lightweight woods good for modelmaking.

Respect the physical properties of the materials you use. Paper shouldn't be asked to support weight; illustration board doesn't like to bend; foamcore will warp; museum board fights erasure. When you pick the right material for the job it will oblige you by behaving well.

Adhesives are essential to modelmaking. These are the basic types:

- White glue (PVA). Sobo and Elmer's are the most common. White glues are water soluble until they dry. Tacky Glue is a white glue that is already partially set up.

- Rubber cement (latex-based glue). Use for paper. Rubber cement is not archival quality; it will discolor paper over a period of years.

- Spray adhesive. Suitable for paper and card. Spray both sides. There is no room for error—once the two sides meet, the join is irrevocable. In a studio environment the drift from spraying may pervade the entire air space. It also enters the ventilation system and is conducted to other areas of the building. The fallout leaves a perceptible residue on surfaces and breathing fumes is bad for your health. Moral: Do all spraying out of doors or in a spray booth.

- Balsa wood cement, Duco, or "magic" glues. These dry quickly and are good for wood and plastic.

- Sticky tape

Other materials mentioned in this book are useful but less frequently used. They include: dry mount (tissue adhesive applied with heat), corrugated cardboard, plywood, particle board (wood shavings pressed into a thick board), wire (steel and copper), electrical wire, monofilament (clear plastic string), clear plastic sheets, plastic screen, steel straight pins, corsage pins, nylon stocking material, cotton knit fabric, wooden dowels, wooden skewers, round toothpicks, plastic straws, Styrofoam balls, wooden beads, loofah sponge, natural sponge, steel wool, cotton wool, dried sedum (a plant with an umbrella-like seed head), sandpaper, spray paint.

GUIDELINES AND TIPS

From the scale drawings to the last tree, take pains to be precise, neat, and careful. To make the modelmaking process smoother:

- Begin your model by making careful orthographic drawings—that is, plans and elevations. Measurements are taken from the plans and elevations, and meticulous attention to both the drawings and the measurements taken from them is essential.

- Use new knife blades and change them often. As blades get dull they tear the material instead of cutting it. Dull blades also cause wear and tear on arms and hands. Wear and tear should not be in the form of blood and tears, either—new blades are extremely sharp, so be careful.

- Always place cardboard or some sort of cutting board underneath what you are cutting. This not only saves the surface of the table but also preserves your knife blades.

- Use the least amount of glue possible.

- White glue can be spread evenly on a surface by using a piece of illustration board as a squeegee.

- Make a habit of using the heavy-duty utility knife for straight cuts. It gives straighter, surer cuts than the skinny craft knife, which is prone to veer. Craft knives are good for details, curves, and very small cuts.

- Always cut against a metal straight edge, because cutting against plastic (T square, parallel bar, or triangle) is guaranteed to ruin your equipment.

- Stand when you cut to exert maximum pressure on the straight edge and the knife.

SIMPLE BASES

Study models do not necessarily require bases on which to sit, but a presentation model needs to have a base in order to be portable. Bases are generally made before construction of the model begins. Simple bases are easiest to make. Contoured bases, which are more complicated, are discussed in chapter 5.

A single sheet of ½" (12 mm) plywood or particle board can be used for a small- to medium-sized simple base, up to 20" by 30" (51 x 76 cm), for example. Single sheets of illustration board, chipboard, or foamcore are not suitable because they will warp. Two sheets of ⅛" (3 mm) chipboard glued together make a firm support. Weight it with a pile of books. After it is dry, the chipboard can be cut with a saber or band saw and the lamination will be almost invisible.

A lighter-weight base can be made like a box (figure 1.6). Illustration board, ⅛" (3 mm) chipboard, and foamcore make good box bases. Cut a bottom piece, top piece, and four sides. For butted corners, remember to cut two of the strips shorter by two times the thickness of the board. One to two inches (2.5 to 5 cm) of depth for the box is

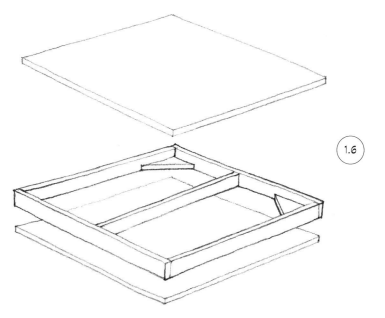

1.6

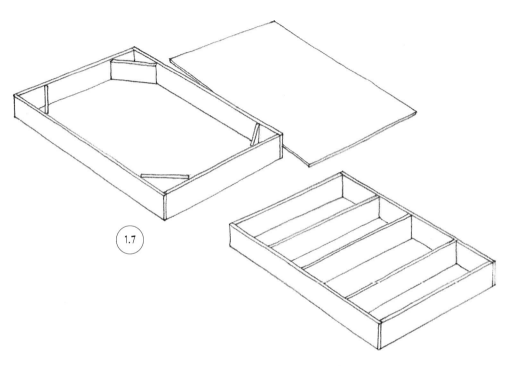

(1.7)

sufficient. You can place the top and bottom pieces on the top and bottom of the perimeter wall, or you can enclose the top and bottom pieces within the perimeter wall. Reinforce the interior of the base with strips of board that are cut to the proper depth and glued in. Angles across each corner or a series of parallel strips provide additional reinforcement (figure 1.7).

Foamcore makes a good box base because it is lightweight. Construct a hollow box with reinforcements and, using rubber cement or spray adhesive, cover it with a neutral-toned drawing paper.

2

Chipboard and
Cardboard Models

Chipboard (pulpboard), cardboard, and other cheap materials like paper, posterboard (instead of illustration board), tape, glue, and paper clips are ideal for making study models, because worrying about expense is inhibiting rather than liberating. Experimentation often produces interesting new directions and solutions. The study model, which may be an end in itself or the preface to a presentation model, is an ideal place to work out problems of volume and scale.

CHIPBOARD MODELS

Chipboard is a cardboard-like material that is cheap, easy to cut, and comes in two common thicknesses: $1/16$" (1.4 mm) and $1/8$" (3 mm). Actually, the single-ply board is $1/24$" (1 mm) and

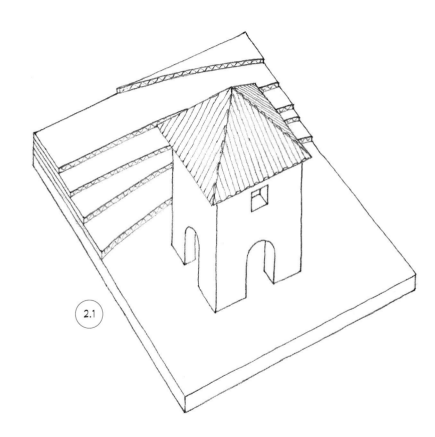

2.1

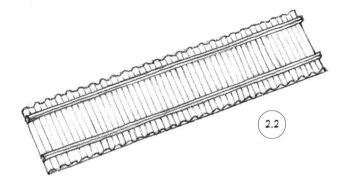

2.2

the two-ply is $\frac{1}{12}$" (2–3 mm), but they are usually referred to as $\frac{1}{16}$" and $\frac{1}{8}$". The most useful is $\frac{1}{16}$" because it is easiest to cut. Generally chipboard is a soft gray or sometimes a neutral tan, the same on both sides, with a matching core. Though usually employed for study models, chipboard can be handsome when it is assembled and detailed with taste and discrimination.

CARDBOARD MODELS

Corrugated cardboard is easy to find and usually free (e.g., grocery cartons, packing boxes). Heavy- and lightweight corrugated cardboards are practical for study models. Used for medium- to large-sized models, cardboard is easily cut, glued, taped, and pinned. Volumes, positive and negative, can be roughed out quickly and changes can be made without losing much time.

Trying to refine cardboard is usually more trouble than it is worth. However, there are some specialty uses that merit attention. Thin cardboard, $\frac{1}{16}$" (1–1.4 mm) for example, is very good for representing a tile roof at $\frac{1}{4}$" (1:50) scale (figure 2.1). Peel the paper layer from one side of the board. Use a knife to twitch off the paper where it sticks. The remaining bits of residue give the impression of an old, lichen-covered roof.

Thin corrugated cardboard also can be peeled and cut to produce reasonable train tracks (figure 2.2). Glue down narrow balsa-wood rods for the rails.

When thin corrugated is used for land contours, its exposed edges give a pleasing degree of texture to the model base (figure 2.1).

Stripped of its cover, corrugated cardboard curves beautifully (figure 2.3), making cylinders, sinuous retaining walls, Japanese bamboo fences, and undulating roofs, not to mention a one-brick-thick serpentine wall like that of Thomas Jefferson at the University of Virginia. If desired, corrugated cardboard may be covered with an appropriate paper.

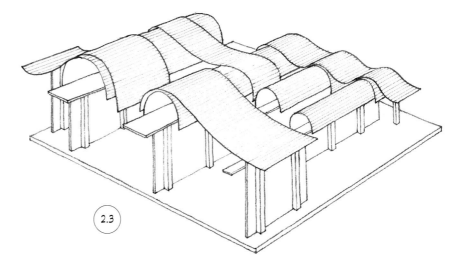

2.3

UNDULATING ROOFS IN THE SPIRIT OF
ANTHONY J. LUMSDEN & ASSOCIATES

3

Paper Models

With a foot in both the study- and presentation-model camps, paper models are becoming increasingly useful as architecture becomes ever more plastic and sculptural. The computer has made it possible to produce working drawings for structures that swoop and soar, penetrate and extrude, defying all the tenets of classicism. In many respects, a material like modeling clay is the best answer for three-dimensional "quick-sketches," despite its drawbacks of weight and oiliness. But paper comes in handy for initial volume studies of nonorthographic shapes. It is bendable, foldable, and pleatable, and it can be cut with scissors and secured with rubber cement, hot wax, paper clips, tape, spit, etc.

The basics of paper models are relatively simple. Many kinds of paper are suitable. Regular bond typewriter or copier paper works well for cylinders and curving surfaces, index card stock is

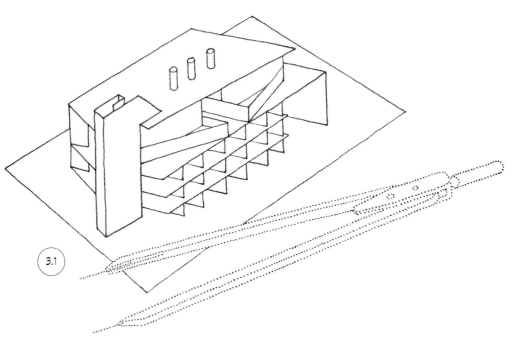

3.1

excellent for small models, and museum board has a pleasing surface. Museum board is generally classified as a heavy-weight paper, though it comes in several weights. Two-ply is commendable for small models. If the paper is thin or the piece is so small that taping on the inside is not practical, flaps can be added to the pattern for sticking the pieces together. Rubber cement and stick glue work well. No water-based adhesives please, because the paper will buckle. If it can be hidden from view, sticky tape is frequently the quickest and easiest solution.

A tiny model about the size of your hand is made successfully with index card, cover stock, or single-ply museum board (figure 3.1). Obviously, only the basic framework—walls, overhangs, and sloping planes—can be shown at this scale.

BOXES

The simple box form is the foundation of most traditional buildings and also of many modern buildings (figure 3.2). A plain box can be made from one piece of paper (figure 3.3). The top,

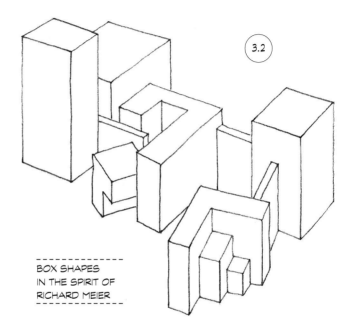

3.2

BOX SHAPES
IN THE SPIRIT OF
RICHARD MEIER

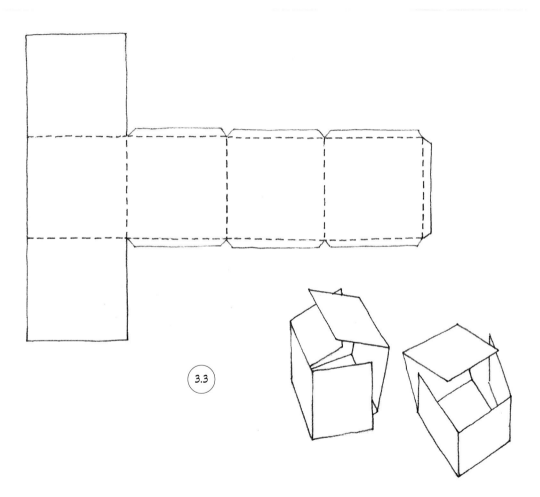

3.3

sides, and bottom are drawn in a row, while the two ends are drawn on either side of the bottom piece.

PITCHED ROOFS

Pitched roofs (figure 3.4) are made with a single fold. Use at least cover-stock or museum-board weight. Take the pitch and height of the roof from the side elevation drawing. Take the length of the roof from the front elevation drawing (figure 3.5). Score the ridgeline lightly and fold (figure 3.6). Scoring helps to produce a clean, accurate fold. If the material is the weight of illustration board, the score can be made with a knife. Make a light cut following the fold line on the front or the back depending on the direction of the fold. It goes without saying that great care must be taken not to cut too deeply. Score paper against a straight edge with the back of a scissors blade, the edge of an erasing shield, or with your fingernail.

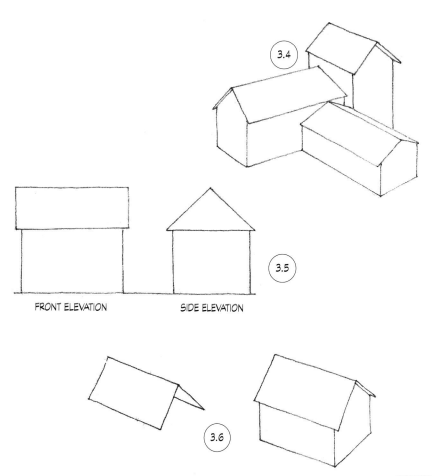

FRONT ELEVATION   SIDE ELEVATION

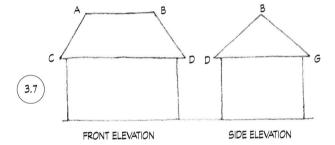

FRONT ELEVATION   SIDE ELEVATION

HIP ROOFS

The only true lines we have in the hip roof elevations are the length of the ridgeline and the length and width of the eave line (figure 3.7). True measurements of the roof slope cannot be taken from the elevations because they slope in two different directions. Bear in mind that in the side elevation drawing, point B can also be point E or point A and that point D can also be point C or F.

Draw a horizontal line that is the measured length of the ridgeline AB (figure 3.8). Drop a perpendicular line from the center point E to F, which will be the length of BD in the side elevation drawing. Through F draw a horizontal line CD, which is the measured length of the roof at the eave line. Repeat this figure as if it were flipped up on line AB.

Construct a triangle on line BG in which BG and BH are the same length as BD and line GH is the measured width of the roof at the eave line (figure 3.9). Add flaps if necessary, fold, and glue (figure 3.10).

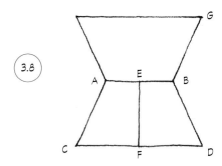

(3.8)

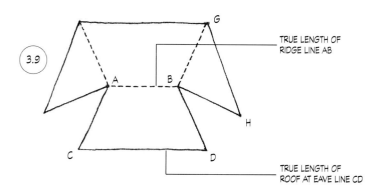

(3.9)

TRUE LENGTH OF
RIDGE LINE AB

TRUE LENGTH OF
ROOF AT EAVE LINE CD

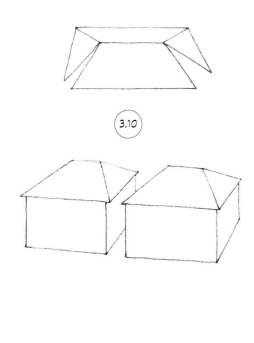

(3.10)

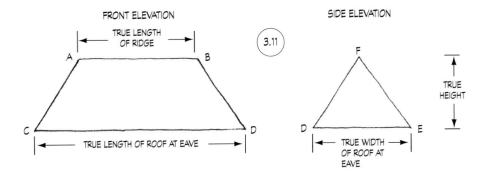

FRONT ELEVATION

TRUE LENGTH
OF RIDGE

A   B

C   D

TRUE LENGTH OF ROOF AT EAVE

3.11

SIDE ELEVATION

F

D   E

TRUE WIDTH
OF ROOF AT
EAVE

TRUE
HEIGHT

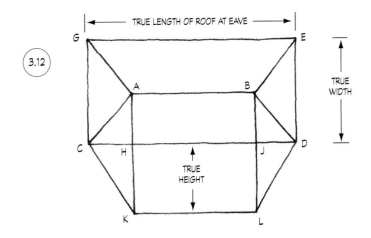

3.12

TRUE LENGTH OF ROOF AT EAVE

G   E

A   B

C   D
H   J

K   L

TRUE
WIDTH

TRUE
HEIGHT

A hip roof can also be made as a solid. Taking the measurements from your front and side elevation drawings (figure 3.11), draw a rectangle to scale that is the length and width of the roof, GEDC (figure 3.12). Inside the rectangle, center the ridgeline AB. Connect A to G and C. Connect B to E and D. Drop perpendiculars from A and B, so that HK and JL are the true height of the roof. Repeat this figure as if it were flipped up on line AB.

Extend A to M and B to F so that MN and OF are the true height of the roof (figure 3.13). Add flaps if necessary, cut out, and glue (figure 3.14).

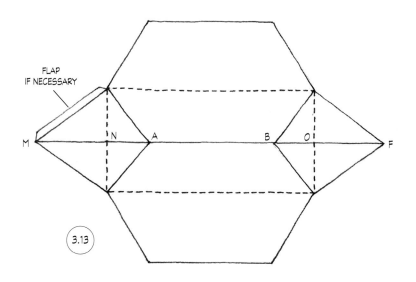

FLAP
IF NECESSARY

M   N   A   B   O   F

3.13

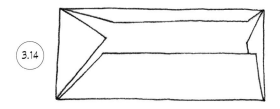

3.14

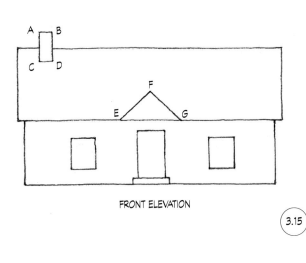

A B
C D

F
E G

FRONT ELEVATION

GABLE RIDGE LINE

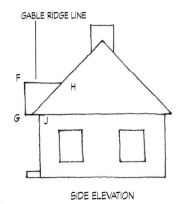

F
H
G
J

SIDE ELEVATION

(3.15)

CHIMNEYS

Take the height and length of the chimney from the front elevation and the depth of the chimney from the side elevation (figure 3.15). Take the angle of the roof pitch from the side elevation. Make the chimney in one piece, folding along the dotted lines (figure 3.16).

(3.16)

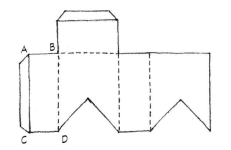

A B
C D

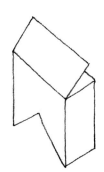

GABLES

Measure the lengths of the two pitches of the gable—EF and FG—and draw them, to scale, as a straight line (figure 3.17). Draw a perpendicular from F to H that is the measured length of the ridgeline of the gable. Draw perpendiculars from E and G to represent the distance the gable extends forward from the eave of the roof, GJ and EK on the illustration. Connect HK and HJ. On line FG draw the triangle EFG that is, in fact, the measured elevation of the gable. Fold on the dotted lines and glue, using a flap if necessary.

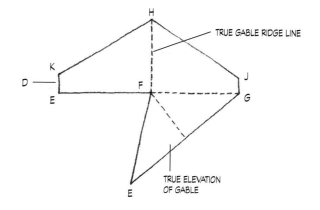

TRUE GABLE RIDGE LINE

TRUE ELEVATION OF GABLE

3.17

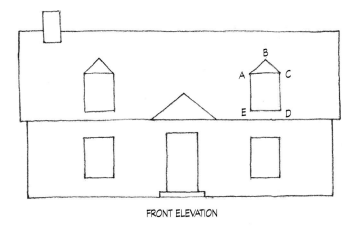

FRONT ELEVATION

(3.18a)

DORMER WINDOWS

Draw to scale the front elevation of the dormer ensemble (ABCDE) (figure 3.18). On side BC, draw rectangle BCGF, which is equivalent to rectangle BCGF on the side elevation. Extend line BF to H and connect H to G. Line BH is the to-scale measurement of the ridgeline. Extend line BC to J, making CJ the same length as CD. Connect J to G. Duplicate the figure (BHGJ) on the other side of line BH.

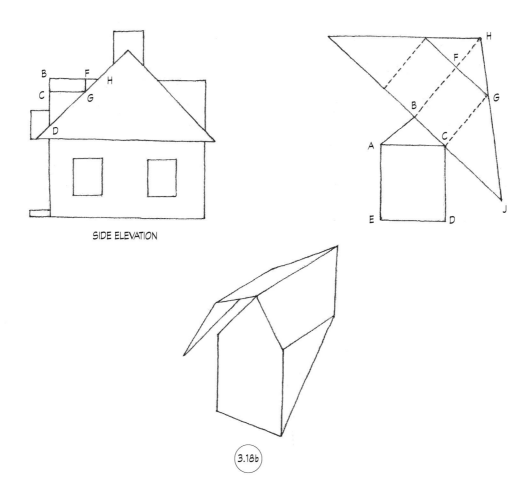

SIDE ELEVATION

3.18b

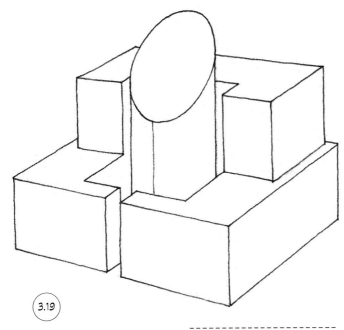

TRUNCATED CYLINDER WITH
SLOPING TOP IN THE SPIRIT OF
MARIO BOTTA

GEOMETRIC AND NONTRADITIONAL SHAPES

Portions of geometric shapes are popular in contemporary architecture (figure 3.19). Prisms, sections of cones, truncated cylinders, amputations of the Platonic solids, sections of spheres—wildly exotic shapes fill the pages of architecture magazines.

Truncated Cylinder with Sloping Top

Draw a side elevation of the proposed cylinder to the proper scale and show the desired slope of the top (figure 3.20). Now measure the height of the tallest part of the cylinder and of the lowest edge of the sloping top. Transfer this drawing to a grid (figure 3.21). Calculate the circumference of the cylinder by multiplying the diameter by π (3.1416). Draw a new grid (figure 3.22) using the circumference of the cylinder as the length. Mark the high and low points of the top of the cylinder, with one or the other at the center of

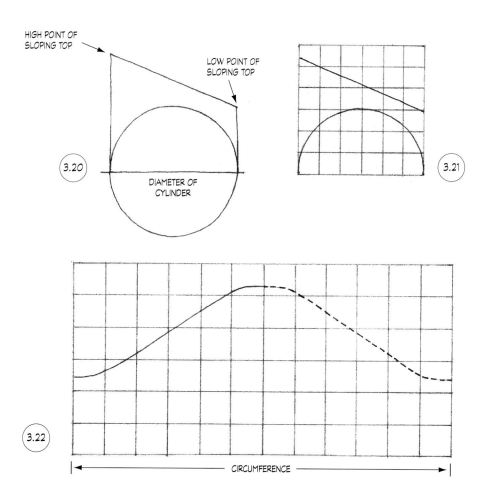

HIGH POINT OF
SLOPING TOP

LOW POINT OF
SLOPING TOP

3.20

DIAMETER OF
CYLINDER

3.21

3.22

CIRCUMFERENCE

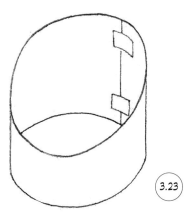

3.23

the line. Connect the points with a straight line that curves gently into another straight line at the position of the high point and the low point. Cut out and tape together (figure 3.23).

For the cylinder's top draw an ellipse with the short direction equal to the cylinder's diameter and the long direction equal to the length of the top's slope. To draw an ellipse: Enclose the area of the ellipse in a rectangle (figure 3.24). Find the center by crossing the diagonals. Bisect the figure lengthwise and widthwise. Fit a curve into each quadrant, touching the outside lines at each bisection. It is best to draw one smooth curve and then trace it to the other three sides. (This is a shortcut to ellipse drawing but is generally good enough to pass muster.)

Cut out the ellipse and tape it to the cylinder at the highest point first. The top will now fold down like a lid (figure 3.25). You may want to add a final step: cut out a paper circle the diameter of the cylinder and tape it inside the cylinder at the bottom to keep the shape properly circular.

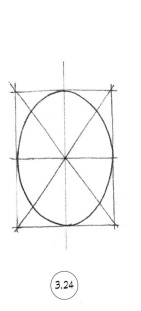

3.24

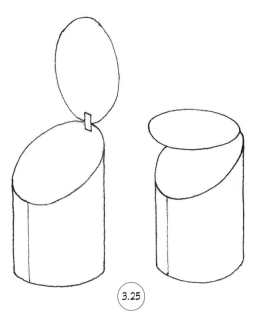

3.25

Truncated Cone with Sloping Top

Cones with sloping tops (conic sections) (figure 3.26) begin with a circular collar and some trial and error. First, cut out a doughnut shape (figure 3.27). Cut the doughnut in half (or less than half) (figure 3.28) and experiment with curling the collar into a cone. Squeeze the half-doughnut sides together and cut the center hole down farther on one side in a gentle curve (figure 3.29). The pattern for the cone will look like figure 3.30.

To make the top, invert the cone and trace around the hole onto a piece of paper. Tape to the high point of the cone first, then bend the top down like a lid and tape again (figure 3.31).

Sails

Modern sail shapes can be made with bond-weight paper (figure 3.32). Since measurements aren't readily adaptable to fluid shapes, patterns are used instead. Patterns can easily be varied in

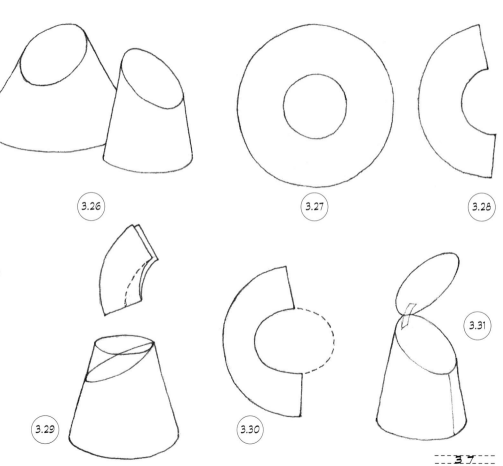

3.26

3.27

3.28

3.29

3.30

3.31

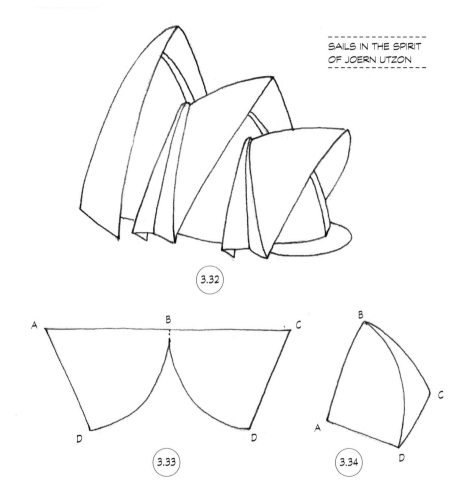

3.32

3.33

3.34

height and width and roundness of curves to fit the desired space. The pattern in figure 3.33 should be folded at B and taped together along the curving edges of BD (figure 3.34).

Figure 3.35 forms a hooded shape to be placed over figure 3.33. Fold at B and tape together the curving edges of BD. Fold under the flaps and tape them to whatever you are using as a base (figure 3.36).

Figure 3.37 is the fan-like pattern for a flange that lies on the back edge of the hood. Notice the angled bottoms to the three strips. This is to allow the flange to rest level on the base even though the flange itself tips in several directions (figure 3.38). Glue or tape the flange to the hood (figure 3.39).

Cut the shapes so that as many segments as possible remain joined at one end. It makes the gluing or taping of curving pieces much easier.

Only trial and error will produce the results that you want, but during that effort some unexpected solutions may present themselves.

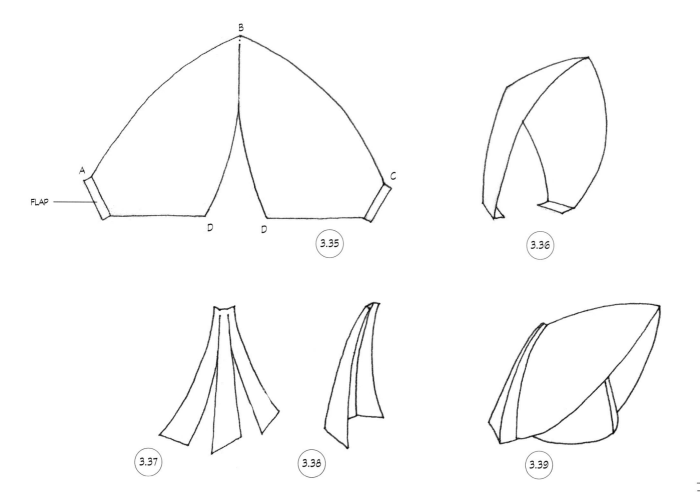

B

A

FLAP

D   D

C

3.35

3.36

3.37

3.38

3.39

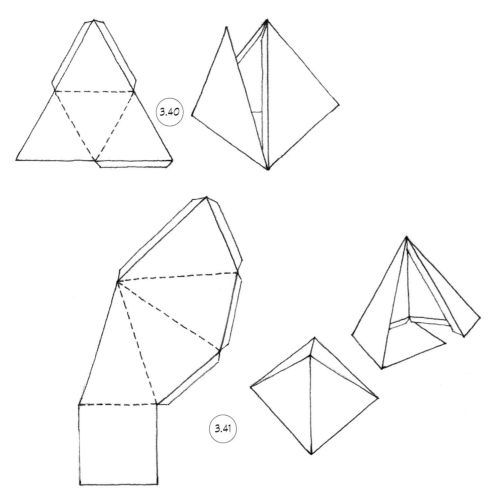

Pyramids

Many contemporary architects exploit geometric solid forms. The pyramid is a popular one. Usually called three-sided or four-sided, pyramids have either an equilateral triangle (three-sided) or a square (four-sided) as a base.

A triangle appears to be a rigid figure because the implied thrust of each side is absorbed by its adjacent side. When a regular triangle is translated into three dimensions it becomes a tetrahedron—a three-sided pyramid—and is rigid, just as each of its faces is rigid. Rigid forms are comforting in models as well as actual buildings because their stresses are internalized and need no supplementary buttressing.

The most obvious pattern for a tetrahedron consists of four triangles arranged to form a large triangle (figure 3.40). If the paper is thin, flaps are necessary for gluing. The apex of a regular pyramid is over the center of the regular-sided base. Pyramids having an apex not over the center of the base are called oblique.

The pattern for four-sided pyramids—sometimes called half octahedrons—has sides joined

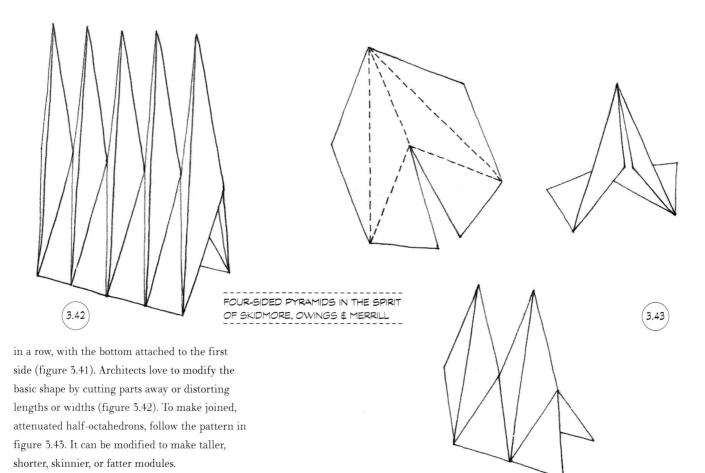

FOUR-SIDED PYRAMIDS IN THE SPIRIT
OF SKIDMORE, OWINGS & MERRILL

3.43

in a row, with the bottom attached to the first
side (figure 3.41). Architects love to modify the
basic shape by cutting parts away or distorting
lengths or widths (figure 3.42). To make joined,
attenuated half-octahedrons, follow the pattern in
figure 3.43. It can be modified to make taller,
shorter, skinnier, or fatter modules.

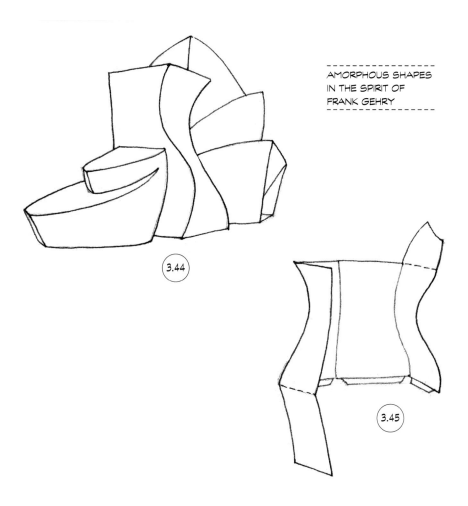

AMORPHOUS SHAPES
IN THE SPIRIT OF
FRANK GEHRY

3.44

3.45

Amorphous Shapes

As those who commission public buildings (particularly museums) are discovering, the envelope can be as great an attraction as its contents. Flamboyant pieces of architecture-as-sculpture are becoming common in avant-garde studios (figure 3.44).

Nothing heavier than bond paper will bend easily enough to model small-scale amorphous shapes. Decide on the shape of the bottom of the structure and draw it. The sides will be by guess and by golly. If the bottom edge of a side piece is straight it can be cut in one piece with the base (figure 3.45).

Tape or dot with instant glue the curving side of piece 4 to one side after another, matching A to A, B to B, C to C, and D to D, before closing and taping the top and bottom (figure 3.46). You may have to draw many study models before you come up with an accurate pattern.

Large models can be made with single-ply museum board and can be glued instead of taped.

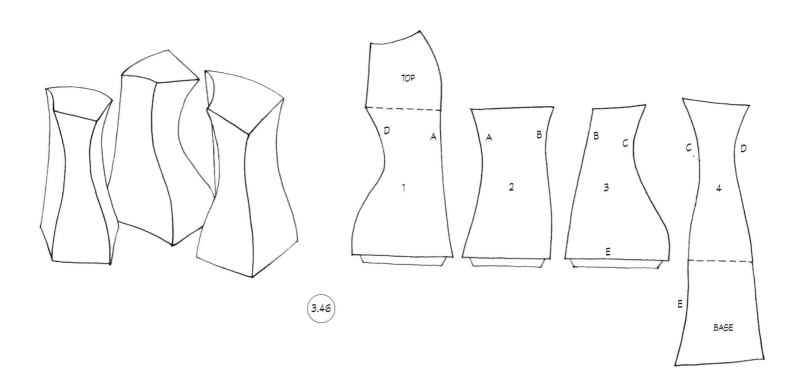

TOP

D   A   A   B   B   C   C   D

1   2   3   4

E   E

BASE

3.46

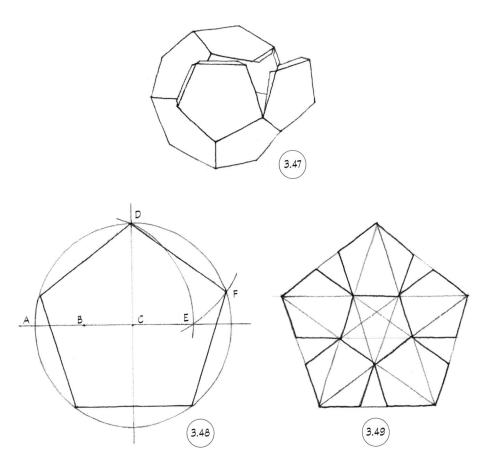

(3.47)

(3.48)

(3.49)

Spheres and Parts of Spheres

Real spheres are not practical to construct, and Styrofoam balls are obviously limited in many ways. But you can approximate a sphere by constructing a figure out of facets. The more facets there are to a given surface, the rounder the object will appear. Two kinds of facets are simple to cut out: pentagons and regular triangles.

Twelve pentagons make a reasonable shape that looks like a soccer ball. It is called a dodecahedron (figure 3.47). To draw a pentagon using a protractor: Divide 360 (the number of degrees in a circle) by five. Draw a circle. Lay the straight edge of the protractor on the diameter of the circle and mark off 72 degrees five times. If you have no protractor, draw a circle and bisect it horizontally and vertically (figure 3.48). Divide line AC in half to make point B. Draw an arc from B whose radius is BD; the arc will cross the diameter line at E. Then draw an arc from D whose radius is DE; the arc will cross the circle at F. The line DF is the length of one side of the pentagon.

A pentagon can also be drawn by using dividers. By trial and error, step off an approximate distance on the perimeter of the circle until you secure five equal divisions.

To build a sphere, draw two large pentagons, each one made up of six small pentagons (figure 3.49). Each large pentagon will be half of the sphere, or a dome (figure 3.50). Use the straight edge and compass carefully—small inaccuracies become large errors when they are multiplied (figure 3.51).

Called geodesic domes or spheres, structures like this were developed by engineer-architect R. Buckminster Fuller (1895–1983). In principle, such domes (half a sphere) distribute the stresses within the structure itself, as in a truss.

More refined pseudospheres are made with regular triangles. Twenty regular triangles make the pattern for an icosahedron (figure 3.52). Add flaps for gluing if it is necessary. For more about domes, see page 62.

Sliced-off or "broken" spheres produce interesting spaces and forms (figure 3.53).

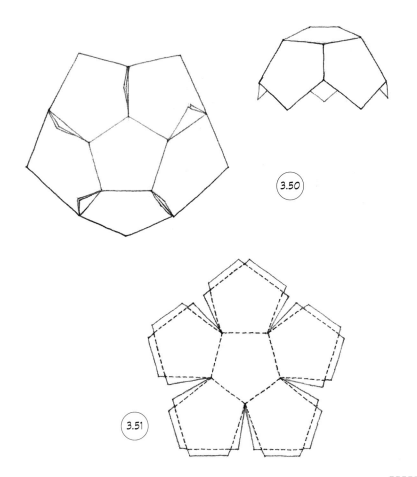

3.50

3.51

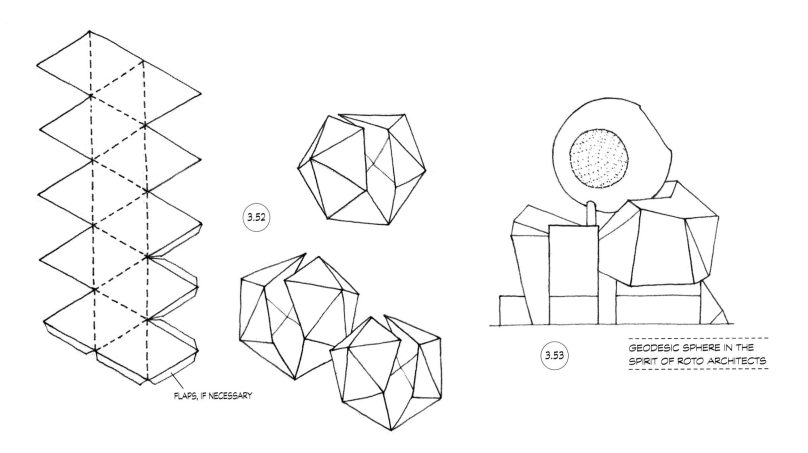

FLAPS, IF NECESSARY

3.52

3.53

GEODESIC SPHERE IN THE
SPIRIT OF ROTO ARCHITECTS

Planes

Contemporary architects enjoy exploiting the sculptural possibilities of walls. In other words, walls are used as large planar surfaces that can be modeled to enhance their dramatic effect (figures 3.54, 3.55, 3.56).

Thick walls with punched windows have a dramatic design impact, particularly when the windows are angled or have sloping sills. Le Corbusier set the standard (figure 3.57).

To make punched windows, cut the window holes in the front wall and the back wall, using measurements from your elevation drawings. Glue the front and back walls to a bottom piece of the proper width, and add a brace to hold things together during assembly of the window (figure 3.58). Taking measurements from the front elevation and from a cross section of the wall, cut out the bottom, top, and sides of the window reveal. Assemble by first gluing in the bottom of the window, then the sides, then the top (figure 3.59).

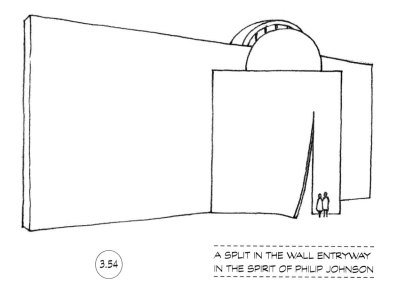

3.54

A SPLIT IN THE WALL ENTRYWAY
IN THE SPIRIT OF PHILIP JOHNSON

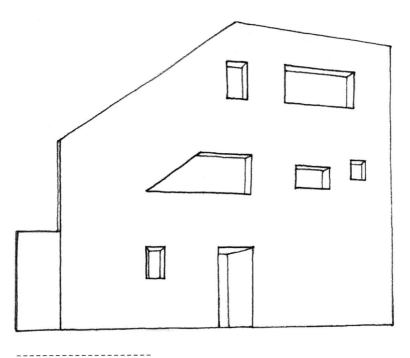

WALL PLANE AS A SCREEN
IN THE SPIRIT OF
ANTOINE PREDOCK

(3.55)

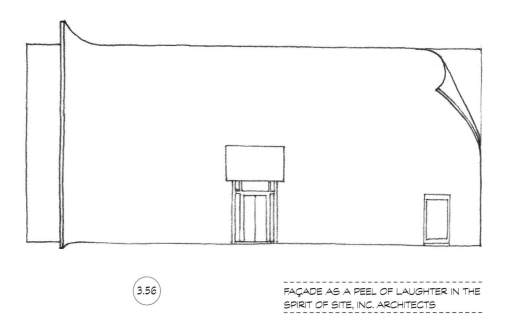

3.56

FAÇADE AS A PEEL OF LAUGHTER IN THE
SPIRIT OF SITE, INC. ARCHITECTS

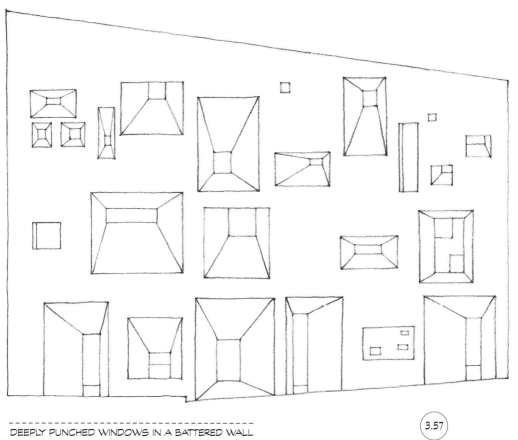

DEEPLY PUNCHED WINDOWS IN A BATTERED WALL
IN THE SPIRIT OF LE CORBUSIER

3.57

The window also can be made as a unit—like an open-ended box—and then glued in place (figure 3.60). Construction is the same if the wall is battered, that is, wider at the bottom than at the top. The pattern for a one-piece open-ended box begins with a cross section of the wall showing the position and size of the window openings. Score and fold the piece and glue into place.

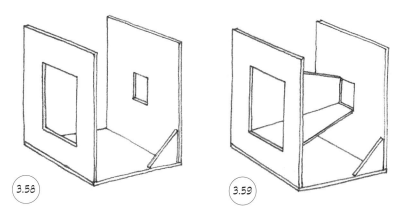

3.58

3.59

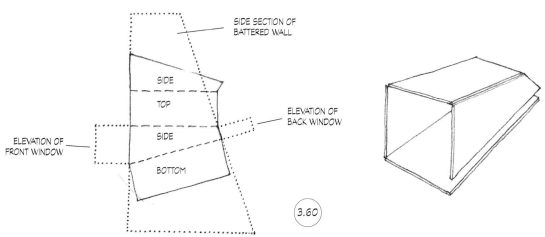

SIDE SECTION OF
BATTERED WALL

SIDE

TOP

SIDE

BOTTOM

ELEVATION OF
FRONT WINDOW

ELEVATION OF
BACK WINDOW

3.60

FAÇADES

Some models depict every detail—fenestration, moldings, bricks, architectural tile, etc.—particularly models of historic buildings, cityscapes, or monuments. Fortunately, a photocopy machine can do the hard part. Photocopy an elevation of the desired façade to the proper scale. Mount the photocopy on the face of the model before assembling the parts. Dry mount is particularly good for small jobs like this, but rubber cement, spray adhesive, or white glue will do (figure 3.61).

If the façade incorporates deeply recessed windows and doors, photocopy two copies of the façade. Mount one on the piece of illustration board that will be the front of the building and cut out the areas to be recessed. Mount the other copy on a similar piece of board. Glue the first sheet on top of the second sheet.

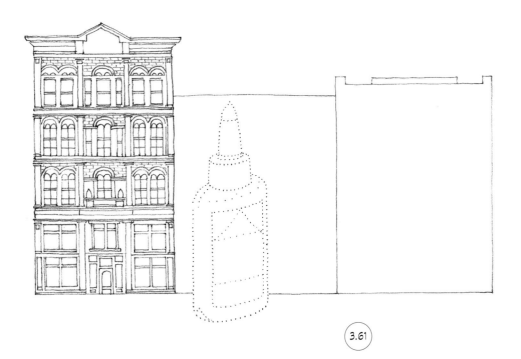

3.61

4

Illustration Board Models

Illustration board, with its cold- or hot-press
finish, makes a handsome model. The texture is
fine grained and hard, and the white surface is
flawless. The back side is a neutral tone, frequently greenish, and the core is gray, necessitating the
covering of joins. Usually $\frac{1}{16}$" (1–1.4 mm) thick,
illustration board is one of the most desirable
surfaces for presentation models.

STRAIGHT CUTS

Illustration board, which is the material of choice
for most models, is fairly difficult to cut. It usually takes several strokes to cut through and with
each stroke there is the possibility of deviation.
You should use the heavy-duty utility knife
because it is less likely to veer than the lighter-
weight craft knife. With it use a metal straight-

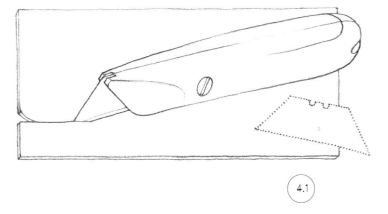

4.1

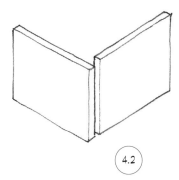

4.2

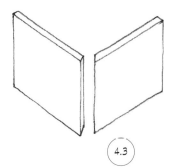

4.3

edge. Most metal rulers have a cork backing that keeps them from slipping and raises them a little, which prevents ink from running beneath the ruler. Unfortunately, it also allows space for the knife blade to veer from the vertical. Using the ruler metal side down prevents this, but you need to put extra pressure on it to keep it in place.

Hold the utility knife vertically and at a very low angle, which helps to keep it straight. Try to cut through the board in one pass (figure 4.1).

CORNERS

Accurate, clean corners are the most important aspect of a good model. There are several ways of making corners when building with $\frac{1}{16}$" to $\frac{1}{8}$" (1.4 mm–3 mm) thick chipboard or illustration board: butting, beveling, bending, and excising. All techniques produce good results; beveling is the most sophisticated.

Butted Corners (figure 4.2)

In a butted corner, the end of one piece of board meets the side of the other piece. It is an easy corner to make but it does leave an exposed edge. In a fine model the edge would be covered or another type of corner would be used.

Beveled Corners (figure 4.3)

Beveling is called for when the core of the board is a different color than the surface. First, learn to use the board cutter with its beveler. For good results, adjust the length of the blade so that it just cuts through the board. Cutting deeper than is needed makes the cut more difficult and dulls the blade. The cutter has a flat guide to keep the blade at the proper angle, and another flat guide to run along the edge of the straight edge. If possible, start the cut $\frac{1}{2}$" (1 cm) before the cut line to allow the cutter to become steady.

Bent Corners (figure 4.4)

Because bending leaves corners with a bite taken out of them, it is generally reserved for structures that meander, like a garden wall, or for angles that are not square (figure 4.4).

To make a rectangle out of one strip, measure each side and subtract twice the width of the board. At the join, bead the glue just on the edge of the join. Do not butt.

Excised Corners (figure 4.5)

Cut a V-shaped slice out of the backside of the fold. It is not as hard as it sounds. Use a metal ruler and allow the knife to angle under the edge at approximately a 45-degree angle, being careful, of course, not to cut all the way through. Turn the board around and make another cut at the same angle. Pick out the fuzz from the cut before folding. This method produces a beautiful corner, with the good paper remaining on the front, although it has a soft edge instead of a razor-sharp one.

Gluing Corners

Cleanliness is next to godliness when you are using illustration board. Keep glue to a minimum and have a paper towel handy to wipe your hands.

When using white glue such as Elmer's or Sobo, drop a blob of glue on a nonabsorptive surface and allow it to begin setting up while you proceed with other steps. You may want to use

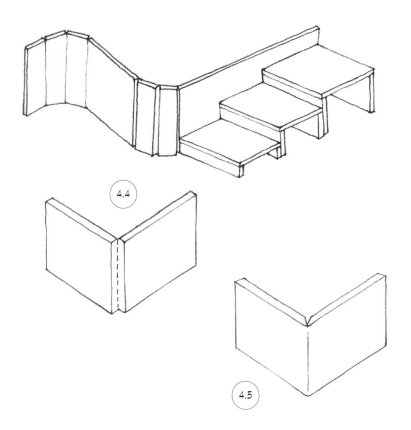

4.4

4.5

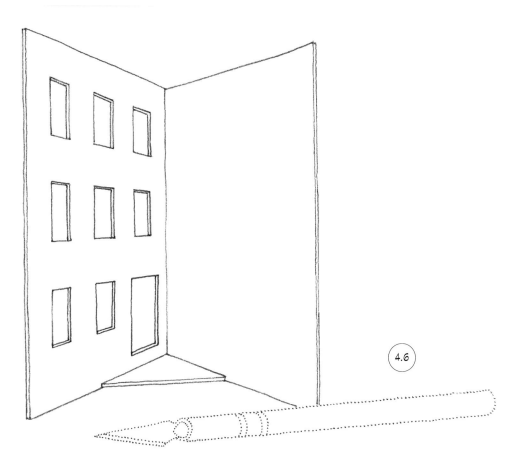

4.6

Tacky Glue, which is already partially set up. Apply glue to the edges and corners by taking some on your finger and drawing it along the backside edge of the board so that it leaves a thin bead along the edge. Use the least amount of glue possible.

WALLS

Using the measurements from your orthographic drawings, draw the north and south walls of your building on the right side of the illustration board. Your drawings should already be the proper scale. A scale of $\frac{1}{8}$"=1' (1:100) works well for small models. Use the utility knife to cut lines as straight as possible.

Draw the other two parallel walls to the proper height. If you are using butted corners, subtract $\frac{1}{8}$" (3 mm), which is twice the thickness of the illustration board, from the lengthwise dimension of the walls.

Before you assemble the walls, doors and windows must be cut (see following section). To assemble the walls, cut off a corner piece (or use your 45°-by-45° triangle to cut a right angle) of spare board to use as a template. Glue your walls together two at a time, holding them in place against the triangle while the glue dries. This will ensure accurate corners. When the four walls are firmly joined together, cut a corner piece of spare board and glue it to an inside corner of the box to give it some strength (figure 4.6).

WINDOWS AND DOORS

All buildings depend on walls; they are the inescapable primary unit of structure. Into the walls go doors and windows, which are, on the outside, mainly aesthetic. In a small model, doors and windows may simply be holes cut in the board (figure 4.7) or they may be drawn on the wall and not cut out at all. Door and window frames may be cut out of a piece of card and glued to the wall, giving it a more three-dimensional look (figure 4.8). Window holes are sometimes enhanced by backing with black paper or, if a greater degree of realism is desired, with thin plastic. Another good effect is obtained by taping a toned paper behind

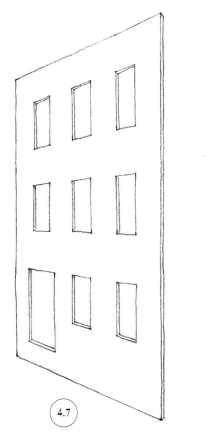

4.7

4.8

the holes. A neutral shade slightly different than the wall color is pleasing. Window mullions (the strips that hold the glass panes in place) can be drawn directly on the board or can be cut out of paper or board for a larger-scale model.

Cut windows and doors in your walls. You should already have decided upon a window technique: cut out entirely; cut out and backed with black paper, thin plastic, or the same board; or drawn on the board. Point the craft knife straight down at the entry spot, then cut. Turn the board and cut the second corner. Touch up the cuts gently with sandpaper or a nail file. If the window openings are large, cut them before you cut out the wall. If you are backing doors and windows with paper, glue it on now.

CYLINDERS

Cylinders and other tight curves are made from chipboard or illustration board by scoring and bending the board (figure 4.9). Scoring produces a pleasing texture. The more scores, the more elegant and smoother the curve, to a point—

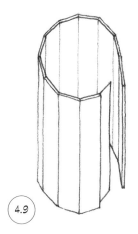

4.9

scores closer together than $\frac{1}{8}$" will begin to split and delaminate.

To make a cylinder, find the circumference of the base by multiplying the diameter by π (3.1416). Cut the illustration board $\frac{1}{4}$" (6 mm) longer than your measured circumference; the spare $\frac{1}{4}$" (6 mm) will be the flap joining the two edges. Next, practice scoring a scrap of board so you know how deeply to cut. Then, measure, mark, and score the lines. Peel the flap's layers of paper away until only the back skin remains (figure 4.10). Now, bead the flap sparingly with glue and attach it to the other side of the cylinder. An alternative to using a flap is to use a strip of board (figure 4.11). Cut the board to the exact height of the cylinder. Glue the strip of board inside the cylinder to cover the join. If your cylinder fits one of the circles in your circle template, use it to hold your cylinder while the glue dries (figure 4.12).

Museum board, which matches white illustration board quite well in terms of color and texture, can be rolled or bent to some extent. To secure a cylinder, glue in a strip of paper the length of the

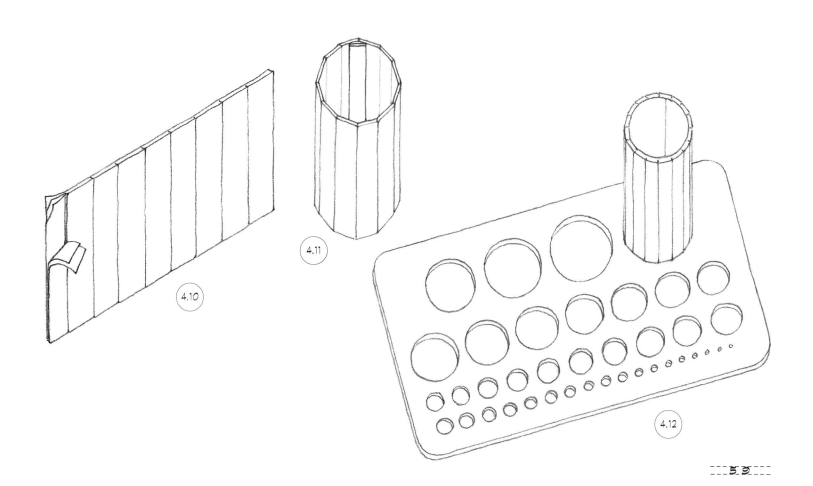

4.10

4.11

4.12

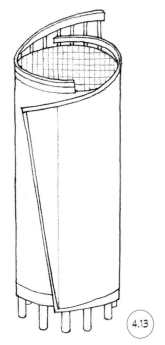

WAVE TOWER
HALF-CYLINDERS IN THE SPIRIT OF
KOHN PEDERSEN FOX ASSOCIATES

4.13

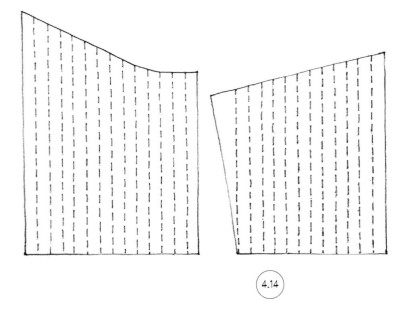

4.14

inside of the joint. Push the cylinder halfway through the hole of your circle template to dry.

There is always the desire to use prefabricated cylinders, such as toilet paper rolls or paper-towel cores, to save time and effort. They must be covered because they are gray or buff and don't look good. Heavy paper does well; rubber cement or spray adhesive will secure the paper. Don't spray paint the tube—the surface is too absorbent and uneven and the results are unacceptable.

As modern architecture has demonstrated, cylinders (and other geometric solids) can be altered in creative and intriguing ways. One example is the wave tower (figure 4.13). To make a wave tower, cut two pieces of illustration board in the shape of the patterns provided and score them vertically every quarter-inch (figure 4.14). Bend the two pieces and glue them together, holding them with clips until dry (figure 4.15). Trace the inside of the bottom of the cylinder onto a piece of board, cut it out, and glue it in the top (figure 4.16). This model is visually effective if the backside of the board with its contrasting color is used for one of the half-cylinders.

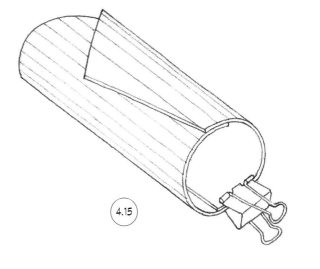

4.15

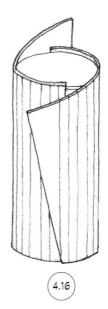

4.16

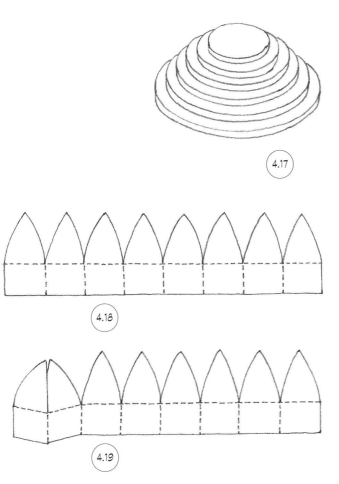

4.17

4.18

4.19

DOMES

Domes are difficult to make. A Styrofoam sphere cut in half may be your best option if using a different material will not spoil the looks of the model. Papier mâché is another possibility.

More often you will opt for a pseudo-dome. Stacking sequentially smaller circles of illustration board is one way to build a pseudo-dome, though small circles are mean to cut (figure 4.17). Cut them out slightly large and then trim them down.

The petal system also produces a pseudo-dome. You need to use sturdy paper, since illustration board is too heavy to bend. Find the circumference of the base and divide it into equal segments. Mark the proper number of segments in a straight line. Make a pattern for a curving petal and trace it onto the segments (figure 4.18). If you leave the bottoms of the petals attached it will be much easier to glue or tape them. The curve of the dome does not start until the petal curves (figure 4.19). Tape the segments together on the inside. Most domes sit on a drum(figure

4.20). Starting the curve slightly above the bottom line produces a drum that can then be covered with heavy paper.

Details can greatly enhance the dome. Cut a narrow strip of lightweight card or cover stock for each joint (figure 4.21). Make them long enough to touch each other at the top. Cut out a collar to encircle the base of the dome, covering the bottom of the strips and the drum (figure 4.22). Add a narrow strip to the collar for more detail (figure 4.23). Make a small collar or drum for a cupola to complete the top. Cut a disk to cover the top of the cupola and finish it off with a wooden bead (figure 4.24).

A ribbed dome is more dependable than the petal form because it has interior support. Draw two circles, cut them in half, and make a notch in each piece. Two halves should be notched at the top and two notched at the bottom (figure 4.25). Assemble the pieces and bend two of the wings into position (figure 4.26). Cut another disk of the same diameter for the dome's base. Glue the ribs to the base, keeping them evenly spaced. The ribs may be covered with three-sided petals that

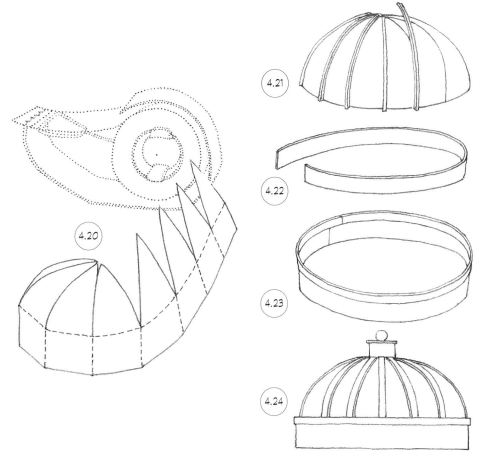

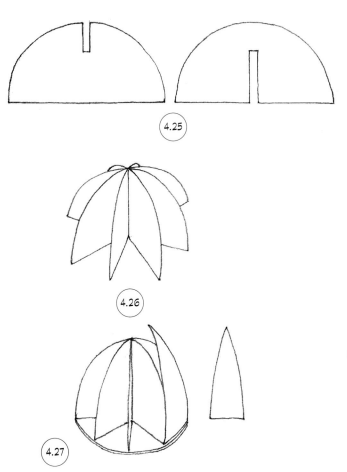

4.25

4.26

4.27

are straight on the bottom and curved on the sides (figure 4.27). Cut a strip of heavy paper to form a collar enclosing the base and the bottom of the petals. The ribs may be left uncovered because they both imply a dome and are exceedingly decorative. More flanges can be used if desired.

A low ersatz dome can be made by cutting a circle out of museum board or sturdy paper (figure 4.28). Cut a radius. Overlap the ends or cut away the overlap. Tape it on the inside.

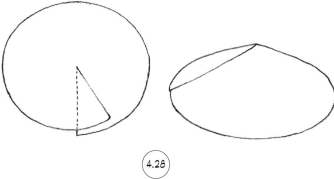

4.28

VAULTS

A barrel vault is a half-cylinder. Its span will be twice its height. Take the measurements of the vault from your drawings. A vault made from one piece of illustration board needs to be attached to walls to keep its shape. A vault with thickness—usually in large-scale models—is made from two half-cylinders and can be freestanding (figure 4.29). Space the two half-cylinders with parallel ribs.

A cross vault is two intersecting barrel vaults (figure 4.30). The intersection of the two vaults creates a complex curve, the construction of which calls for fancy mathematical footwork. An adequate result can be achieved by following the basic shape of the pattern shown (figure 4.31).

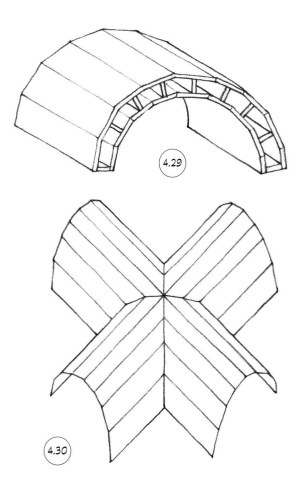

4.29

4.30

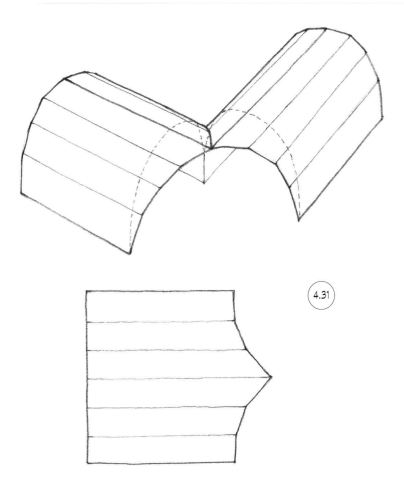

(4.31)

STAIRWAYS

In a study model, a stairway can simply be a sloping ramp. Draw lines on the ramp to indicate stairs. Presentation models, however, must incorporate treads and risers. Check the drawings to determine the overall height of the stairway. As a rule of thumb, stairs have a 7" (18 cm) rise and 12" (30-cm) deep treads, but variations that don't exceed the building code are allowed. Divide the height of the floors by seven to figure out how many stairs to make. Draw the stairway in plan, as though it has been flattened out. Show both the treads and the risers and add one additional riser to be glued to the second-floor plane (figure 4.32). Cut the stairs in one piece out of illustration board, scoring each step alternately on the front or back.

Depending on their length, stairs need one or two stringers for support. Stringers are the framework that support the stairs (figure 4.33). One in the middle will do if the staircase is short. One on either end is needed for wide stairs or for a higher

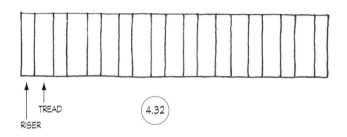

RISER

TREAD

4.32

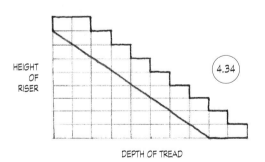

HEIGHT
OF
RISER

4.34

DEPTH OF TREAD

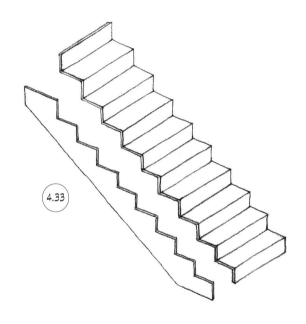

4.33

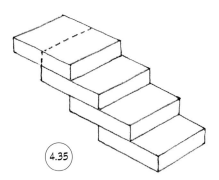

4.35

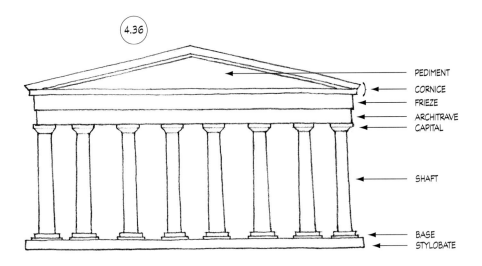

4.36

PEDIMENT
CORNICE
FRIEZE
ARCHITRAVE
CAPITAL

SHAFT

BASE
STYLOBATE

degree of finish. The measurements for the stringers are the same as for the stairs (figure 4.34).

Better-looking stairs can be made by using a material that is the proper scale for your model. Chipboard that is $\frac{1}{16}$" (1 mm) thick will simulate stairs with a riser of 6" (15 cm) in a $\frac{1}{8}$" (1:100) scale model. Laminating two pieces will suit a $\frac{1}{4}$" (1:50) scale model. Cut out each stair separately, doubling its depth to allow it to be glued to the next stair. Glue the final stair under the floor plane of the second floor (figure 4.35).

CLASSIC DETAILS

Simplified versions of classic details can easily be cut out of illustration board. Roman temple façades, much in vogue even now for banks and other public buildings, comprise several distinctive features: a pediment, cornice, frieze, architrave, porch, and columns, which can be further broken down into the capital, shaft, base, and stylobate (figure 4.36). The steps, columns, pediment, and the space behind to the wall of the building make up the porch.

In a model you can simplify the porch by excluding the capitals and bases and by combining the frieze and the architrave. Columns present the biggest problem, because they should be smaller at the top than the bottom and, even more troublesome, should swell in the middle. Since this is well nigh impossible to duplicate in a model, use instead simple cylinders or dowels. Draw vertical lines on the shaft to represent flutes.

To give the frieze a more finished look, add triglyphs and metopes, which are a sequence of three narrow rectangles separated by a space (figure 4.37). Similar to the triglyph and metope is the frieze of dentils, a very simple pattern of alternating rectangles and spaces (figure 4.38).

Other common details are the so-called egg-and-dart motif (figure 4.39) and the Greek-key design (figure 4.40). The Greek-key is easily constructed on a 9-by-10 square grid. In Renaissance architecture, Greek-key and egg-and-dart designs are usually a strip of detail under the cornice and above the frieze, but in revival styles, they can be used almost anywhere that enhancement is desired.

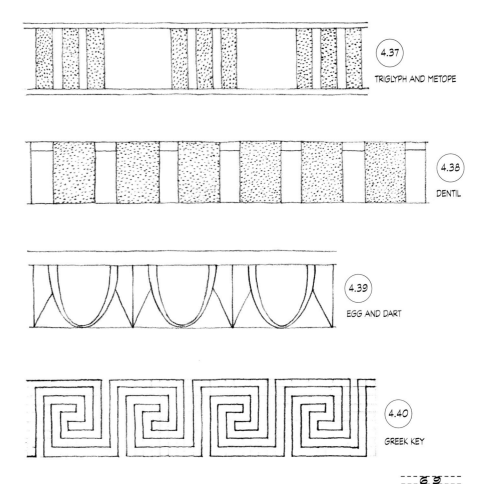

4.37 TRIGLYPH AND METOPE

4.38 DENTIL

4.39 EGG AND DART

4.40 GREEK KEY

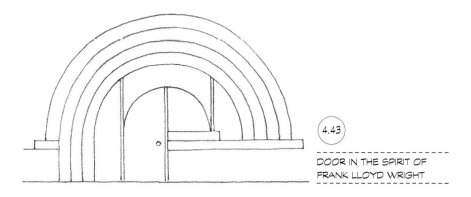

AMERICAN COLONIAL-
STYLE DOOR

4.41

ROMANESQUE
PORTAL AND
WINDOW

4.42

DOOR IN THE SPIRIT OF
FRANK LLOYD WRIGHT

4.43

Renaissance and Baroque designers were pioneers in squashing the porch flat against the front of the building. This makes the modelmaker's job much easier since the various elements, columns included, can be cut out and glued to the wall. When columns are attached to a wall they are called "engaged." A small, simple, American Colonial doorway (figure 4.41) is an example.

Pediment, columns (flat, not rounded), and the single step can be cut from one piece of board. First, establish the number and the order of the layers that you want. If desired, some of the details can be drawn on the board instead of cut out. Notice that in pedimented units the pediment and columns—either freestanding or engaged—protrude farthest and that in all units the door itself is the most recessed part.

In a large Romanesque doorway the porch front (i.e., the square top, its arch, and the connecting columns and the lowest step) can be cut from one piece of board. The inner arches and steps can be drawn on the board for a recessed look (figure 4.42). These examples clearly show the skeletal remains of the classic façade.

The Frank Lloyd Wright storefront (figure 4.43), with its Romanesque roots, is made by drawing the four outer arches and the section of wall they intersect on one piece of board, and setting back the round-topped door as deeply as possible.

Aside from scale, windows and doors are similar in Romanesque, Renaissance, and Baroque designs (figures 4.42, 4.44, 4.45). Tops of the vestigial porch can be pediments, arcs, or arches (figure 4.45). In doors that marked honorific entrances, architects of the period threw caution to the wind and elaborated richly on the traditional Roman style. The English version is outstanding (figure 4.46); the Italian more controlled (figure 4.44).

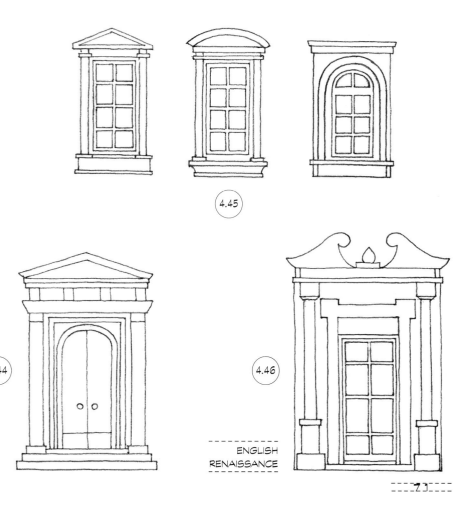

4.45

4.44

ITALIAN
RENAISSANCE

4.46

ENGLISH
RENAISSANCE

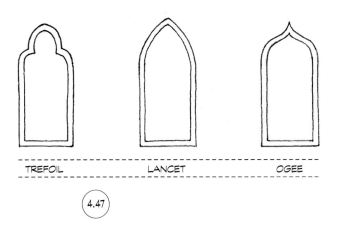

TREFOIL   LANCET   OGEE

4.47

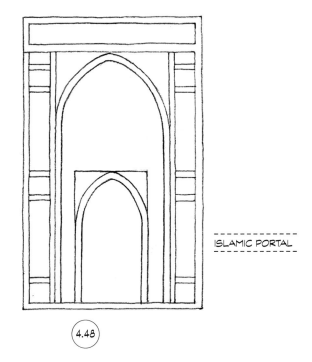

ISLAMIC PORTAL

4.48

OTHER DETAILS

Many other common details can be applied to
your model to establish an architectural period.
Gothic window frames—the lancet, the trefoil,
and the ogee (figure 4.47)—are easily cut out. In
Islamic design, an enormous rectangular frame
dwarfs a smaller arched doorway (figure 4.48).
Japan's mystical relationship with the circle is
often evidenced in their architecture (figure 4.50).

In the twentieth century no styles are sacro-
sanct. Postmodernism has mixed and matched
details ranging from the ancient world to the
future. Arches, arcs, pediments, columns, dorm-
ers, domes—all are combined without regard to
consistency or provenance. Hans Hollein's door
(he has made his reputation on inspired
entrances) incorporates bits of Eastern culture
(figure 4.49), as does Issiki's reference to an
ancient Japanese moongate (figure 4.50). Steven
Holl's carefully placed and varied rectangles of
glass recall the Bauhaus and Piet Mondrian (figure 4.51). There is room for everything in eclecti-
cism.

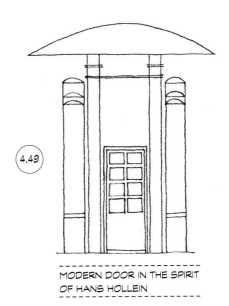

4.49

MODERN DOOR IN THE SPIRIT
OF HANS HOLLEIN

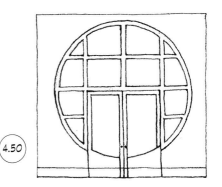

4.50

JAPANESE-STYLE DOOR IN THE SPIRIT
OF ISSIKI ARCHITECTS

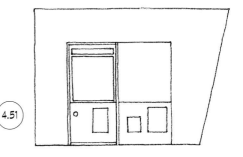

4.51

MODERN DOOR IN THE SPIRIT OF
STEVEN HOLL

5

Contour Bases

LEVEL SITES

An architectural model may simply describe and define a building or it may include the site. The word *site* implies measured areas of differing topographies. If the site is level, the model will sit on a flat piece of board, reinforced if necessary to keep it from warping. To give a slight three-dimensional effect, two layers of card can be used. First, cover the whole base with a piece of card of the chosen color. Glue it down and weight it until it is dry. This surface represents the street and driveway level. Next, cut sidewalks, lawns, and planting beds out of another sheet of card and glue them onto your base. This provides just enough difference in elevation to clarify the land use without distracting from the architecture (figure 5.1). Architects prefer neutral tones or white for the entire model ensemble—build-

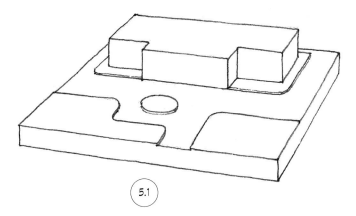

5.1

ings, site, entourage, and planting. Landscape architects, on the other hand, endeavor to put a more realistic face on models. They often color coordinate the layers, using, for example, a greenish board for lawn areas, gray or white for driveways and streets, and brown for undeveloped land.

SIMPLE CONTOURS

If the site has a simple sloping contour, the slope can be incorporated into the base. Slope is identified by rise (height in feet or meters) and run (horizontal distance in feet or meters). A one-in-ten slope would be a rise of one foot over a distance of ten feet. It would be drawn on a grid, with the rising line defining the contour (figure 5.2). Rise divided by run equals the percentage of slope. A 100-percent slope results from a rise that is equal to the run. On a grid this would be represented by a 45-degree angle.

To create a base that incorporates slope (figure 5.3), draw at least three contours to scale and cut them out of illustration board. Mount these on the bottom piece of your base. The two outside

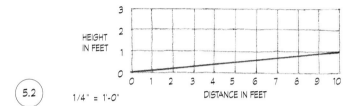

5.2

HEIGHT IN FEET

DISTANCE IN FEET

1/4" = 1'-0"

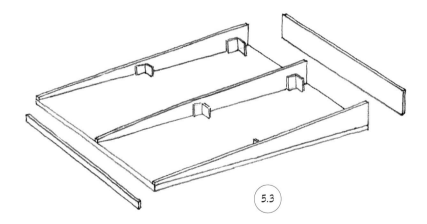

5.3

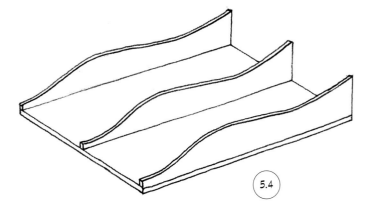

5.4

contours should be even with the outside edges of the base. Cut out strips to cover the high and low ends of the base. Reinforce the contour strips by gluing scored and folded pieces of illustration board against them.

Any contour that does not curve too tightly for the illustration board to bend and that proceeds as a contour in only one direction can be made in this fashion (figure 5.4).

COMPLEX CONTOURS

Complex contours are built up in layers of illustration board, chipboard, cardboard, or a material that approximates the thickness, to scale, of the rise in contour. For example, ⅛" chipboard is the proper thickness for the contours of a ⅛"=1' model. Each layer represents a rise in height equal to one foot. The stepped effect of a contoured site has a pleasing design quality and is an easy-to-understand shorthand for land forms.

Since contours represent a rise in ground level over a certain horizontal distance, it follows that the fewer the contours, the less the slope. Like-

wise, contours closer together translate as a steep-
er grade. Contours never cross each other. For
vertical bluffs, retaining walls, or foundations,
the contour lines will fall on top of each other.
Contour lines are usually labeled according to
their elevation in feet (or meters) above sea level
(figure 5.5). On an architectural plan the contours are marked outside the site boundaries and
should be marked on both ends of each contour
line (figure 5.6).

Architectural models and their sites are measured on an architect's scale, which is calibrated
in feet and inches: $\frac{1}{2}''=1'$, $\frac{1}{4}''=1'$, $\frac{1}{8}''=1'$, etc.
(or, on a metric scale, 1:20, 1:50, 1:100, etc.). The
scale has two calibrations on each of its three
edges, one starting at each end. Be careful to use
the correct set of numbers. Measurements begin
at zero, not at the end of the scale.

Landscape architects, who usually deal with
much larger sites, use an engineering scale calibrated in decimals, varying from ten to the inch
to sixty to the inch. A landscaper's plot plan
might be $1''=20'$ (1:200), for example, while an
architect's site plan is scaled at $\frac{1}{8}''=1'$ (1:100).

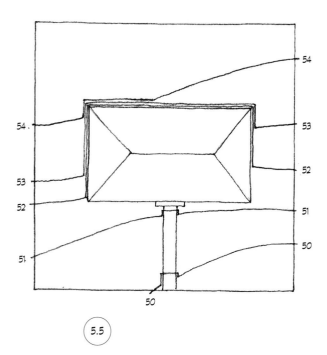

5.5

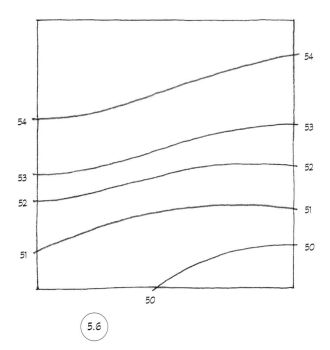

5.6

The vital contour information comes to the model-maker by way of a topographical map or the results of a survey.

To make a contour base you will need at least one copy (or two, to be on the safe side) of the original contour drawing. One of them will be cut up and used as a pattern. To make the copy you can take the easy road to the photocopy machine or you can use the "black the back" technique. To black the back, use a very soft pencil to cover the back side of the vellum with a layer of carbon. Position the vellum, carbon side down, on a sheet of paper and trace the contour lines, transferring them to the paper underneath.

Solid-Core Contour Bases

With solid-core contour bases, each contour is cut so that it covers the whole base behind the contoured edge. This arrangement gives maximum strength, does not need a supplementary piece of board underneath, and is very easy to make.

Using one of the photocopies of the contour drawing, number each contour in order according to the elevation. Cut off each contour and use it as a pattern for the leading edge of its corresponding layer. The rest of the layer will fit the back and sides of the base. Glue and weight them with books until dry. When the base is dry, turn it on its side and trace the stair-step edge onto a piece of illustration board. Cut it out and use it to cover the laminated edge of the base (figure 5.7). Do this for all four sides.

Hollow Contour Bases

The solid-core base is so simple, efficient, and easy that other solutions sometimes seem superfluous. However, the compelling reasons for an alternative are cost (the solid base takes a vast amount of material) and weight (the solid base can become leaden). The alternative is a hollow base, in which the contours are like shelves supported by piers (figure 5.8).

Using one of the photocopies of the contour drawing, label each contour from bottom to top by the elevation number and cut them out (figure 5.9). Start with the lowest contour and trace

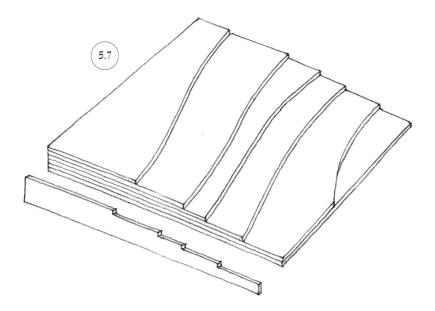

5.7

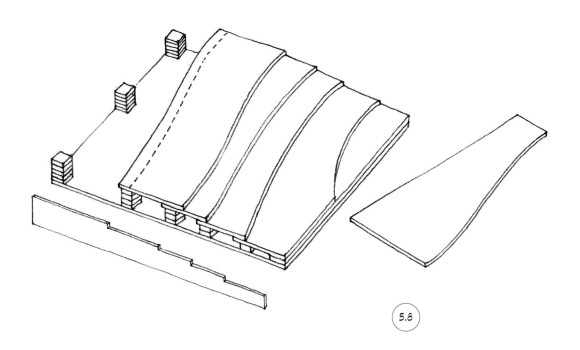

5.8

its outline on a sheet of illustration board. Add a half-inch to an inch (1 to 2.5 cm) to the back edge for overlap (indicated by the dashed line in figure 5.8). Cut out the shape. Trace the outline of the next contour on a piece of illustration board and add a half-inch to an inch (1 to 2.5 cm) to the back edge. Cut out. Continue with each contour.

To create piers, cut a strip about an inch (2.5 cm) wide out of the scrap illustration board. Chop the strip into small squares, and then stack and glue the squares. Start assembling the contours from the lowest elevation. One at a time, glue each contour and its piers and let dry (see figure 5.8). A hollow model needs to be assembled either on a base piece of illustration board or on a previously prepared sub-base.

When the base is dry, turn it on its side and trace the stair-step edge onto a piece of illustration board. Use it to cover the exposed side of the base. Do this for all four sides.

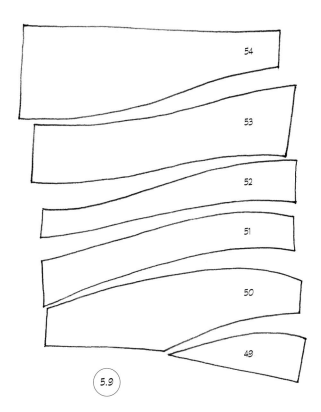

5.9

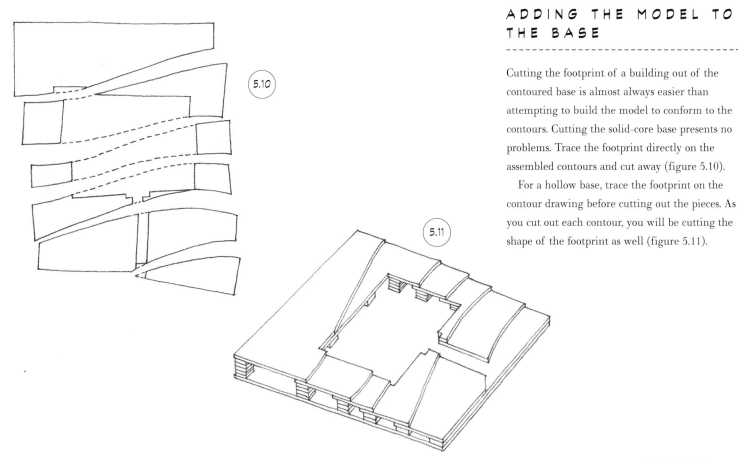

5.10

5.11

ADDING THE MODEL TO THE BASE

Cutting the footprint of a building out of the contoured base is almost always easier than attempting to build the model to conform to the contours. Cutting the solid-core base presents no problems. Trace the footprint directly on the assembled contours and cut away (figure 5.10).

For a hollow base, trace the footprint on the contour drawing before cutting out the pieces. As you cut out each contour, you will be cutting the shape of the footprint as well (figure 5.11).

6
Foamcore Models

The angularity and unadorned robustness of today's architecture are qualities that foamcore handles well (figure 6.1). It is too thick ($\frac{3}{16}$" and $\frac{1}{4}$" [3.5 mm and 5 mm] are common thicknesses) for small-scale models and those with fine detail or embellishments, but it is good for models that demonstrate volumes and broad planes. Some remnants of the brutalist style are still evident in contemporary architecture—features like flat, bare walls, no overhangs, frameless windows, and punched openings. These characteristics are cleanly modeled in foamcore (figure 6.2).

Foamcore has a slick, shiny paper surface, which can be appealing, but it does not take pencil well and is very difficult to erase. Another drawback is that the exposed cut edges are sometimes unattractive. The sharpest of blades is essential for cutting foamcore, as its fill material balls up very easily. If this happens you will be

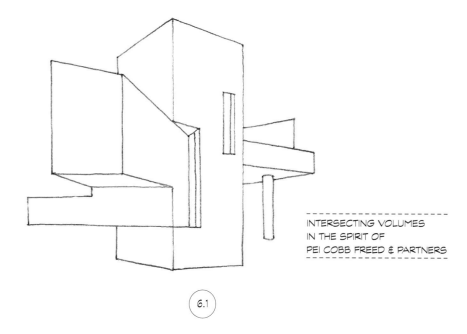

INTERSECTING VOLUMES
IN THE SPIRIT OF
PEI COBB FREED & PARTNERS

6.1

6.2

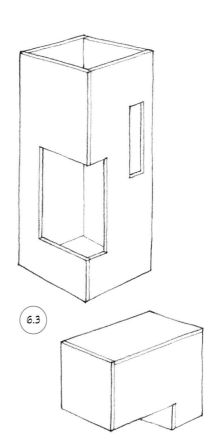

6.3

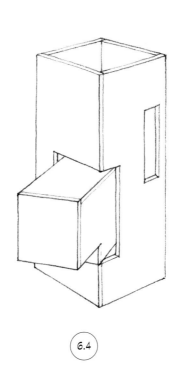

6.4

forced to cover the cut edges, and if you cover one you need to cover all. Cut strips of white paper and glue them on the edges. Beveled corners look very good in foamcore; use the board cutter to make them. Curving surfaces need to be made of an alternative material.

A complex model can be built in separate units that fit together wing by wing or, in modern architecture, units that intersect or overlap. Build the model in distinct parts, with each intersecting unit separate (figure 6.3). Then assemble them (figure 6.4). Freestanding walls can be pinned from the bottom, through the base. If the design has already been formulated there will be drawings from which to take measurements. If the model is the design originator, begin by exploring the possibilities with paper and tape. You will eventually come up with a pattern that can be traced onto the board.

7

Balsa and Basswood Models

Balsa and basswood are similar soft, light-weight woods. Basswood is slightly denser. Balsa wood is often chosen as a presentation model material because it is beautifully textured, lightweight, honey colored, and easy to cut. Since its edges never need to be covered, it makes elegant land contours, terraces, and baronial flights of stairs (figure 7.1). Square and round rods of balsa or basswood are available at crafts stores, and flat sheets come in varying thicknesses. Although thin sheets can be scored and bent slightly, curves have to be made from multiple facets of wood glued together. Of course, another option is to resort to different materials.

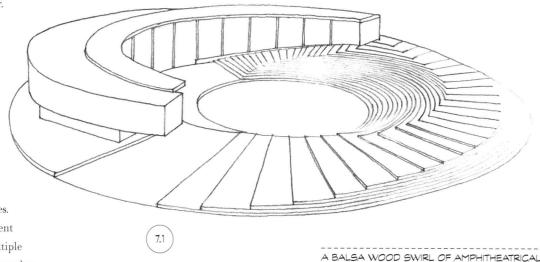

7.1

A BALSA WOOD SWIRL OF AMPHITHEATRICAL SEATING IN THE SPIRIT OF
HAMMEL GREEN & ABRAHAMSON

A wealth of materials can enrich the looks of a wooden model. Architects, who are otherwise notoriously reluctant to make models look "real," enjoy the judicious use of metals and plastics. You can use clear plastic for skylights, windows, water, etc. There are infinite choices for special effects: wire, bent tin, thin copper, metal grids, plastic screening, and BB-shot are just a few possibilities. Use other woods, too. Pine skewers and dowels match balsa in both color and texture. In a $\frac{1}{8}$" (1:100) scale model, $\frac{1}{16}$" (1–1.5 mm) square balsa rods make reasonable columns for a country cottage (figure 7.2). All rods and poles should be recessed into the base.

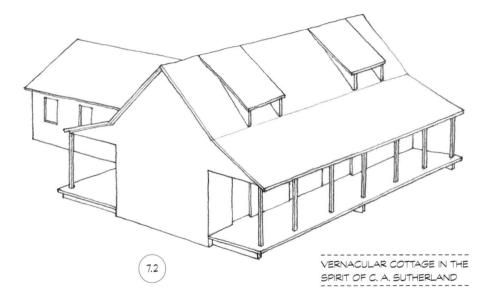

7.2

VERNACULAR COTTAGE IN THE
SPIRIT OF C. A. SUTHERLAND

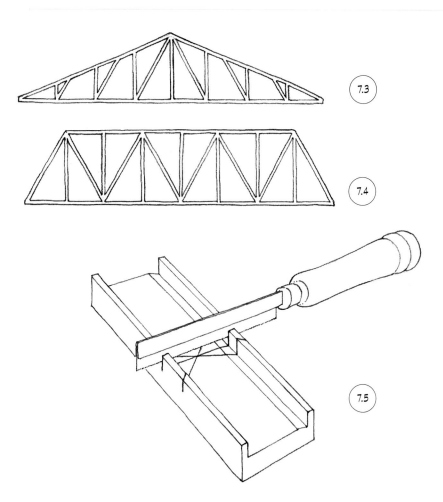

7.3

7.4

7.5

TRUSSES

The *Encyclopedia Britannica* defines a truss as a "structural member usually fabricated from straight pieces of metal or timber to form a series of triangles lying in a single plane." Many little pieces of wood are necessary to make trusses and only using a soft material like balsa or basswood keeps this from being a nightmarish task.

Trusses come in a variety of designs, the most common being the Pratt and the Warren systems. In the Pratt truss the sloping members are parallel to each other on either side of the center (figure 7.3). In the Warren truss the sloping members alternate directions along the length of the truss (figure 7.4). Normally the joints are stabilized with bolts, rivets or welds; for a model, glue will do.

An inexpensive plastic mini-miter box makes truss construction easier. It cuts angles of 90, 45, and 30 degrees (figure 7.5). The razor saw that is used with the box can cut wood, plastic, and soft metals such as brass and copper.

SPACE FRAMES

According to Fuller Moore in *Understanding Structures,* "space frames are three-dimensional truss systems spanning two directions, whose members are in tension or compression only." Essentially, they are a series of openwork pyramids with bases oriented alternately up and down. As roofs, space frames can span large areas economically and gracefully. A half-octahedron module is ideal for covering rectangular spaces because it has a square base.

The frame is made of chords and struts. The chords form the right-angled grids that are the base of the pyramids. The pyramids are made up of struts.

Begin by drawing a square grid to the proper scale on a piece of paper. Cut square or round balsa wood rods to the right size and assemble them on top of the grid, securing the intersections with a blob of glue (figure 7.6). Cut the struts. Each strut should be the same length as one side of one of the squares forming the grid.

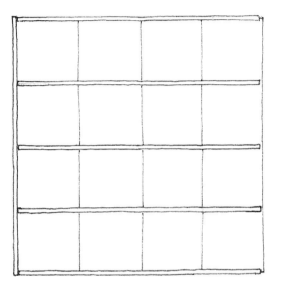
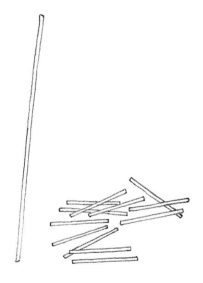

7.6

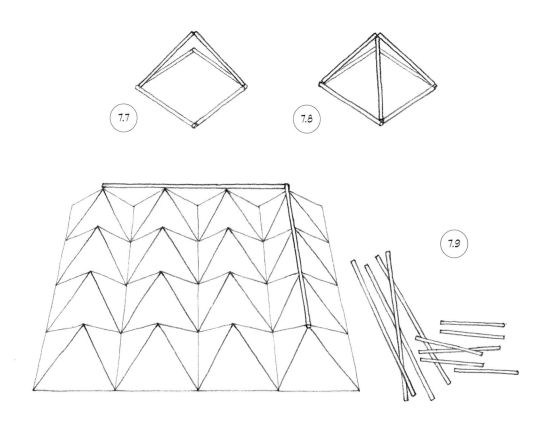

7.7

7.8

7.9

Construct the pyramids by gluing two struts to opposite corners of one of the squares. Lean them together and blob with glue at the top (figure 7.7). Using two more struts, follow the same procedure on the opposite corners (figure 7.8). Repeat for every square. When the whole set of pyramids has dried thoroughly, blob the apex of each pyramid with glue and attach another set of chords, forming another square grid (figure 7.9). Don't worry if some of the apexes don't quite meet the chords. The space frame should be supported at the four corners, with the small grid facing down (figure 7.10).

A DELICATE BALSA MODEL OF AN OUTDOOR THEATER IN THE SPIRIT OF PIERRE THIBAULT

7.10

8

Tents

All structures are in a state of compression and/ or tension. Tensile buildings embrace the genus tents and sails and rely on tension to carry their loads. Tent forms consist of a frame over or under which is stretched a membrane. Its structure is the tent pole and its taut lines. The covering is the fabric membrane.

Visually, the tent is the ultimate in airy romanticism, and the variety of its design is dazzling. The Denver airport is an example of the mountain peak look (figure 8.1). The friendly armadillo look can be seen in the Venafro Laboratory (figure 8.2). The Camp de Mart sports the giant insect look (figure 8.3). As more membranes impervious to the elements are developed, the field for tensile buildings will expand.

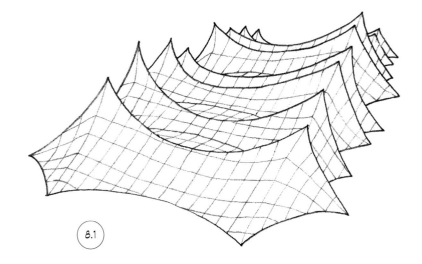

8.1

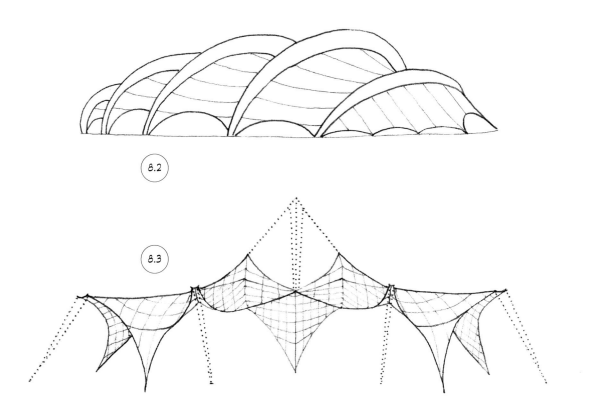

8.2

8.3

MATERIALS

Use foamcore as a base for tensile buildings. It is easy to stick pins into and its thickness allows dowels and heavier pieces to be inset without necessarily having to be glued, thus facilitating possible changes.

There are many choices for the center mast—dowels, plastic straws, wooden skewers, heavy wire. Thin wooden skewers are an excellent choice because they are strong, have a pleasant color and texture, and are up to 12 inches (30 cm) long. They also have one pointed end to stick into the foamcore, and they cut easily with cutting pliers. Aesthetically, the radial poles should be more slender than the mast. Long pins can be used, as can round toothpicks. Round toothpicks, which are fatter in the middle than at the ends, help to keep the fabric from slipping down. They are pointed at each end, so the top pokes neatly into the fabric and the bottom pokes neatly into the foamcore. Making a preliminary hole in the foamcore helps to keep the toothpick from break-ing as you insert it. Use the dividers or a craft knife to punch the hole.

Pins have several functions. Short straight pins can hold the fabric flush to the base. Corsage pins—about 2½" (6 cm) long—can support the fabric well above the base. Corsage pins have a decorative end—little balls, or teardrop-shaped beads—that can become part of the design or can be snipped off. If the fabric is slipping down the pole, secure it by applying a drop of white glue to the underside of the fabric with a toothpick.

Fabric can be any stretchy knit-type cloth, such as T-shirt material or nylon stockings. T-shirt material makes an opaque tent while nylon has a transparent quality. Stockings have certain assets—they are available in a variety of colors, particularly nice neutrals—and they are strong and conform wonderfully to surface contours. T-shirt material sometimes curls, generally the wrong way, on the unsupported edges.

CENTER-SUPPORTED TENTS

The simplest tent form is a center-supported circle or rectangle of fabric stretched by angled poles (figure 8.4). On a piece of foamcore, draft a circle of the appropriate size and divide it into eight equal sections. These will mark the positions of the radial poles. Using the end of your dividers, punch a hole in the center of the circle to facilitate pressing in the center pole. Cut a piece of nylon into a circle and mark the center. Position the center on top of the pole, pick up an edge of the nylon with a pin, and stick it into the foamcore at one of the section marks. Stretch and pin down the opposite side. Continue pinning the fabric on alternate sides until the entire tent is stretched. At that point, all the pins can be adjusted for more or less tension. If the fabric is pinned flush to the base, part of the pin will protrude through the bottom of the foamcore. Trim it off with cutting pliers. When the tension has been adjusted the points can be sewn down and

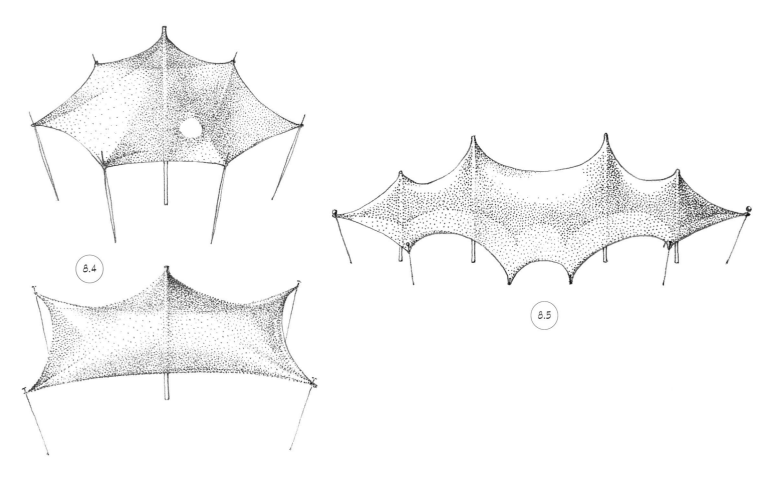

8.4

8.5

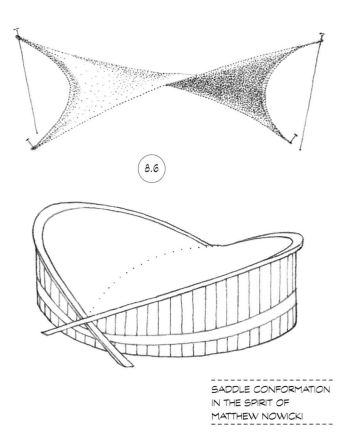

(8.6)

the pins removed. A heavy needle pierces foam-core easily. The resultant look is clean and neat.

More complicated forms have multiple masts and can be varied by raising or lowering the height of the pins (figure 8.5).

SADDLE-SHAPED TENTS

A tent with no internal or external skeleton is formed by pulling up two opposite corners of the fabric and pulling down the other corners. This shape is called a saddle surface (figure 8.6).

ARCH-SUPPORTED TENTS

Arches are another support for the membrane (figure 8.7). They can be cut out of $1/8$" (3 mm) chipboard or two pieces of illustration board glued together. Thin wooden skewers bend, with care, as tight as a $2\frac{1}{2}$" (6 cm) chord and make elegant arches. Heavy wire also will do; anything that holds its shape under the pressure of the fabric is a possibility.

Press the feet of the arches into slits in the foamcore. Don't worry about the lateral stability of the arches—the membrane will hold them in place. A stronger geometry can be achieved by using thread to tie down the valleys between arches. Using a needle, pull the thread through the foamcore and secure it with tape or a drop of glue.

ADDITIONAL SHAPES

A useful shape is the "bandstand shelter" form (figure 8.8). Cut a half-circle out of illustration board and an oval shape out of nylon. Glue one curving edge of the nylon under the curving edge of the board. When dry, glue the board to the foamcore base. Insert the feet of an arch into the foamcore at either end of the half-circle. Pull the nylon up and secure it to the arch by sewing, or glue it by dragging a bead of glue along the arch and then stretching the nylon over it. The elasticity of the nylon will hold it in place while the glue dries. Trim the excess nylon away with small scissors.

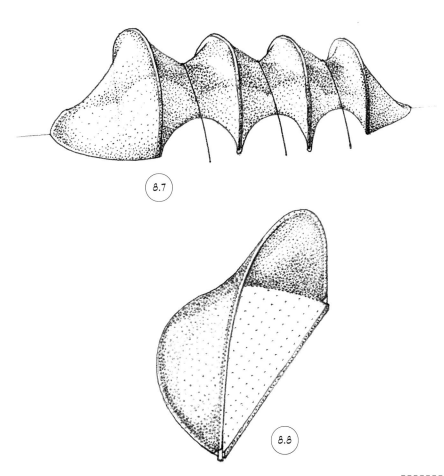

8.7

8.8

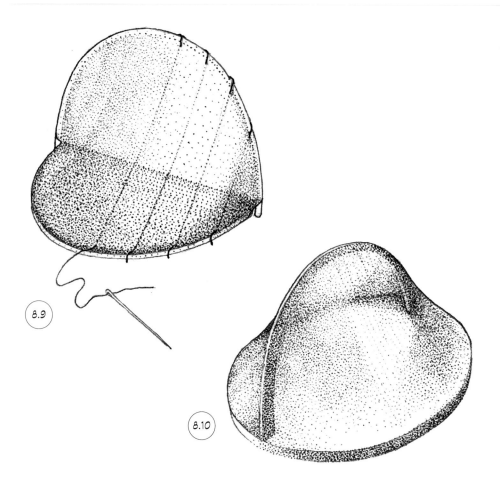

8.9

8.10

This shape can be articulated in an interesting way by using heavy thread for a ribbed look (figure 8.9). With a stout needle and thread, poke the needle through the bottom of the foamcore to come out just outside the curving edge of the illustration board. Do not attempt to go through illustration board with a needle—it is too difficult. Secure the thread on the back of the foamcore with a piece of tape. Take the needle through the nylon close to the illustration board and pull the thread up to the arch, under the nylon. Make it as tight as desired, loop the thread around the arch and advance half an inch (1 cm). Take the thread down to the base, go through the nylon and through the foamcore, move on half an inch (1 cm) and repeat the process, keeping the thread underneath the nylon.

Another shape (figure 8.10) is made by cutting a disk out of illustration board. Make an arch that almost spans the diameter of the disk and insert it into the board. Cut out a circle of nylon for the membrane. Stretch it as tightly as possible over the arch and secure it on the back of the illustration board with glue. Tape the nylon in several places to hold it in place while the glue dries.

For yet another shape (figure 8.11), bend two skewers into similar arches and insert them into a foamcore base. Sew a rectangle of nylon across the top two-thirds of the arches. Tie a thread to the top of each arch to serve as a guy. Pull the arches apart to stretch the nylon and pin the guys down. Always pull the thread through the foamcore base and tape it on the bottom; it makes for an uncluttered, professional-looking model.

EXTERNAL-SKELETON TENTS

Tensile membranes may be stretched to an external skeleton instead of supported by an internal one (figure 8.12). Fix the arch feet firmly in the foamcore. Guy the arch on either side with thread, if necessary. Cut a rectangle or oval of nylon and sew it to the arch, dropping the thread down to allow the pleasing scalloped edge to show under the arch. Pin or sew the tensile points of the nylon to the base.

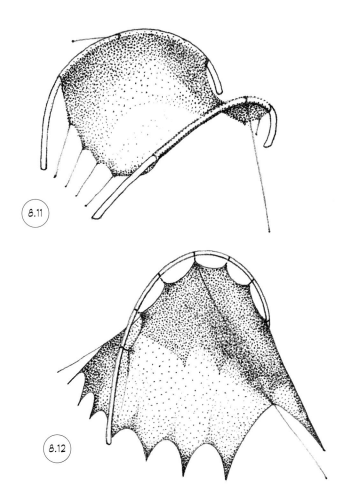

8.11

8.12

9

Entourage

The word entourage, from the French for "sur-
roundings," refers to almost everything that is
not the land or the building itself. Customarily
however, trees, hedges, and people are called
trees, hedges, and people, and entourage is used
for cars, lampposts, benches, water fountains, and the like.

   Entourage is either realistic or
abstract. Architects favor abstract more
often than landscape architects, whose
objectives in designing a model are
quite different. Architects prefer abstraction
because it is undemanding and, if the scale is
right, it does not divert attention from the building. Using abstract forms also helps to achieve
consistency, which is usually a virtue in architectural models. Conversely, in landscape architecture the aim is to show off the arrangement and
diversity of plant forms. The degree of abstraction should correspond to the model. For

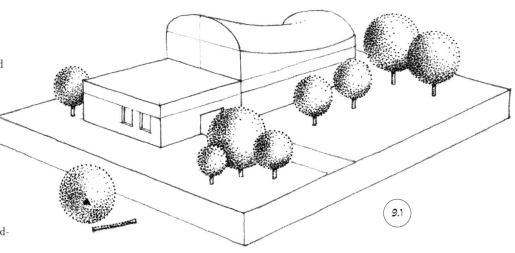

9.1

instance, geometric tree and hedge shapes, which suggest generic plant life, might be used for an all-white model, which suggests a generic building material.

TREES

- -

Geometric Trees

Geometric tree shapes are easy to make and complement monochromatic models. Balls-on-sticks are the quickest solution (figure 9.1). Styrofoam balls come in many diameters. Press a dowel or wooden skewer into the ball and sink the other end into the model base. Ping-Pong balls on round toothpicks can be used too. Styrofoam balls can be painted or sprayed, but test your paint first.

Cones-for-trees can be made of paper (figure 9.2). Start with a half circle, cutting it away until it is the right size. Canson paper is ideal for stylized trees; its weight is perfect and it comes in a rainbow of colors, of which the neutrals are particularly pleasing. Avoid bright

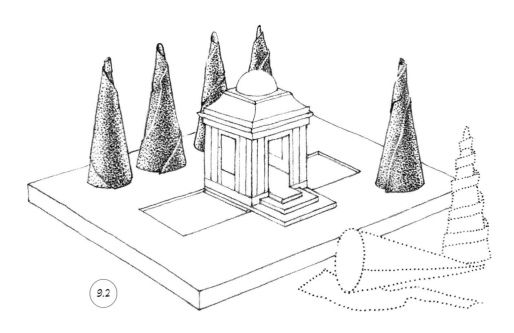

9.2

green. An irregular piece of matching paper wrapped around the cone gives it some subtle texture.

Cone shapes imply all kinds of evergreens and topiary. Balls imply shade trees. Boxes create a formal effect—pleached hornbeam, or, as in France, trimmed chestnuts and sycamores (figure 9.3). Make an open-ended box out of paper. The open end should be square. Glue in a dowel and mount on the base. Use cylinders for poplars and cypresses.

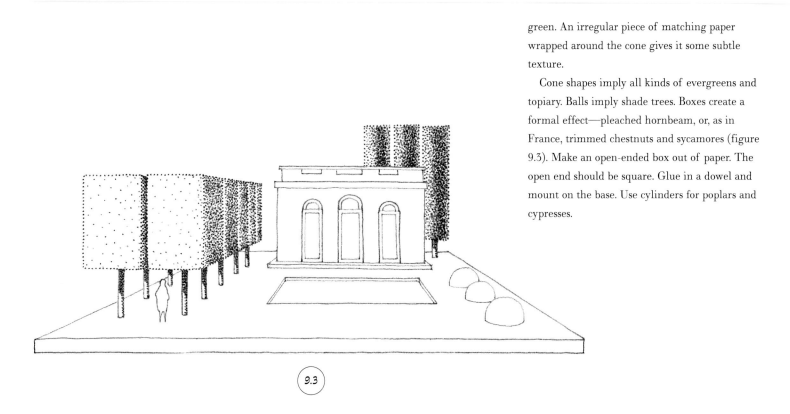

9.3

Material-Based Trees

There are many nongeometric approaches to abstract trees. One favorite is fine steel wool pulled out in a shapely manner and stuck on a dowel or a forked wire (figure 9.4). Its low-key pewter color goes well with all-white or neutral-toned models. Cotton wool is used in the same way. If the cotton is too white, lightly spray it. Crumpled tissue paper is another choice. Sponges are remarkably foliage-like when scissored to the proper shape (figure 9.5). Whiffing sponges with spray paint lends them a luminous quality. For example, pale gray sprayed lightly on a mellow yellow sponge harmonizes wonderfully with a balsa wood model. All of these solutions can be duplicated successfully in small and large sizes, meaning that the trees and shrubs can maintain consistency by using the same vocabulary.

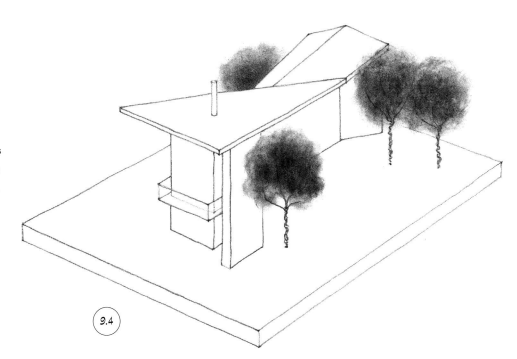

9.4

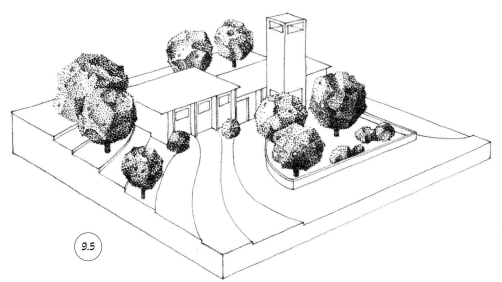

9.5

Wire Trees

Wire trees enjoy a certain popularity. Because their canopy is open, they don't obscure the all-important building. There are countless ways to make wire trees (figure 9.6), but the idea is to bunch together a number of strands of medium weight wire and wrap them with another strand for the trunk, then flare out the filaments to simulate bare branches. Use loops of wire to represent a tree with foliage. Though it is expensive, copper wire is a good choice because it is pliant and easy to cut. It also looks lovely with a wooden model. A piece of electrical wire is a package inviting use. Cut the piece of wire to the proper length. Strip away the insulation, leaving a small amount at the bottom to hold things together while you form the tree. Twist the filaments together if they are not already twisted and then fan out the top (figure 9.6, top right). Trim the wires with scissors if necessary.

Photographic Trees

Black-and-white photos of trees can be photo-copied onto stiff sheets of clear plastic and cut out. Don't attempt to follow the intricate outline of the foliage; cut a simple shape around the outside edge. If the trunk isn't rigid enough to support the tree, glue a wire to it. A variation on this approach is to cut out two identical images, slit them vertically halfway, and slide them together at right angles (figure 9.6, bottom left).

"Flat" Trees

The "flat" three-dimensional look also works (figure 9.6, bottom right). Cut out regular or irregular shapes in diminishing sizes to simulate horizontal sections of tree canopy. Poke a dowel through the centers and secure with a drop of glue.

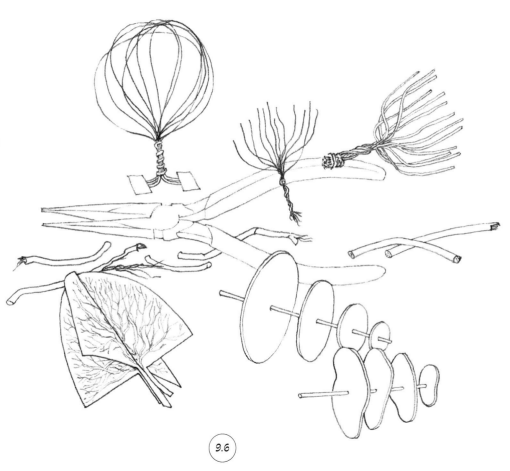

9.6

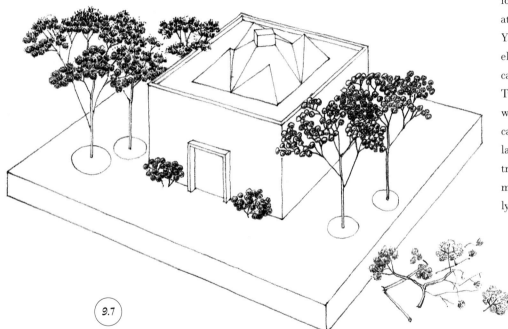

9.7

Realistic Trees

Under the heading of realistic trees come plant forms, which, when dried, are among the most attractive of solutions to the tree (figure 9.7). Yarrow is common and looks like an American elm. Dried sedum is equally good. Any plant that can be dried and that won't shatter is fair game. Twigs that have branched neatly and evenly work well for the deciduous look. All of these examples can be spray painted to match the model or, for landscape architecture, to suggest a species of tree. You can, of course, buy realistic-looking miniature trees at a crafts store, but they are costly and not necessarily better.

SHRUBBERY

Landscape architects call hedges "clipped walls." Living, green, and kinetic in life, they are static and unexciting shapes to model. Sponge is a reasonable answer. Real sponge is better than plastic because it has textural variations that liven it up a little. A whiff of spray paint can help. Loofah sponges are organic material with a prominent, uniform texture and can be cut into a hedge shape. There is also Oasis, the green-block stuff florists use, which is rather crumbly but easy to cut.

Hedges can also be made of paper. If you are making an architectural model, matching the material of the trees with that of the shrubbery is desirable. Canson paper is good for this. Cut out a little texture here and there to relieve the uniformity of the hedge (figure 9.8).

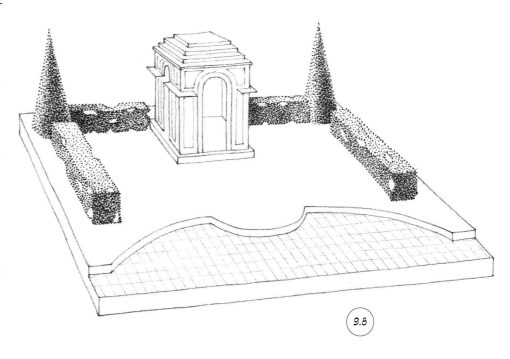

9.8

TEXTURE

Landscape architects are called upon to be specific in identifying areas of living and nonliving forms that appear in a model. Textures drawn on the board are one way of responding to this need. These can range from squiggles and curls to crosshatch and stippling, each designating a species of plant or some change in the surface material. Varying color is another way of indicating change. Colored paper, watercolor, pastel, felt-tipped markers, and spray are some of the many choices. A legend making the distinctions clear should accompany the model. Sandpaper, which comes in varying weights, can signify sand, gravel, or concrete with aggregate. Sprayed green it can become grass or low ground cover.

Some specialty papers are printed to look like wood, stone, marble, and water. A drawback to printed paper can be scale, which may not be close enough to what you need.

Water is an important component of landscape design. Pieces of clear plastic on top of a dark-blue or black base give the appearance of reflective water. A thin layer of Tacky Glue on Canson paper makes a modestly shiny surface that looks wet. A tiny piece of mirror recessed into the board is an excellent pond. Be careful with mirror, though—too much is distracting.

Fountains are a common concern. Sometimes a cluster of thin wires inserted into the base and fanned out can suggest a water jet. Monofilament, a semitransparent plastic thread used for fishing lines, can be used the same way, although its factory curl often has a will of its own.

Agitated water can be simulated with tiny drops of white glue or Duco on clear plastic. White fingernail polish will form nice little dots too. Clear nail polish dripped and dried on plastic leaves a beautiful transparent ring like a soap bubble.

FIGURES

Including people in a model gives it scale and a sense of animation. There are many ways to make figures, ranging from cutting out photographs to total stylization (figure 9.9). The problem with realism, as always, is that models are not the real thing, and the attempt to render them as such is difficult and misleading. For instance, if you use a photograph, do you include both the person's front and back? There is no easy answer. Stylized figures range from recognizable to bizarre. Simple shapes are always acceptable.

Paper Figures

Realistic shapes usually do best in silhouette. They should be monochromatic—black, white, or neutral—and devoid of all detail. To create realistic silhouettes, trace interesting figures out of a magazine and adjust the size on the photocopy machine. Cut the figures out of poster board, cardboard, or cover stock (depending on the scale)

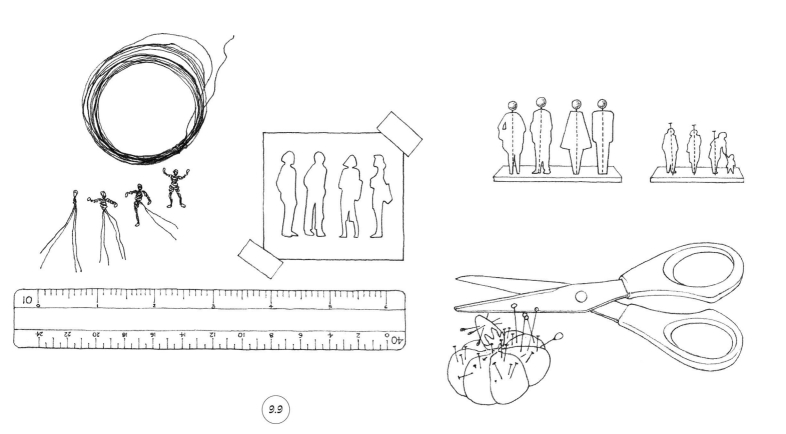

9.9

that is the same color on both sides. Leave a tab on the bottom to stick into the base. If the card is heavy enough, a straight pin can be inserted vertically through the figure and the point pressed into the base. Clip off the head of the pin with pliers.

Diagrammatic shapes, like the international symbols on restroom doors, are also a good solution. If the scale is right, pins with beads on the end can do double duty: the bead forms the head, and the pin, carefully threaded through the card, serves as the support.

Wire Figures

Wire figures are commonly used. If the trees or other parts of your model are wire, figures made of wire will harmonize well. The weight of the wire is determined by the size of the figures. It is not uncommon to need to devise figures barely over a half-inch (1.3 cm) tall.

Use about 20 inches (50 cm) of 30-gauge wire and needle-nosed pliers. Cut the wire in half, fold each piece in half, and twist them together at the top, forming two loops that represent the head and neck. If needed, squeeze the head together and fold it over to make it more bulky. Use one wire for each arm. Fold the wire at the approximate arm length and twist it. Use the rest of the arm wire to twist around the trunk of the body. Use the remaining two wires for each leg. One leg at a time, fold the wire up at the proper leg length and wind the wire around the thigh area to give it some weight. Any leftover wire can be taken down a leg and poked into the base for support.

Other Figures

There are myriad ways to make figures. You can use paper matches: cut and split the cardboard to form legs and leave the head for a head. Wrap pins with yarn. Whittle wood. Cut and bend tin. Any solution will do as long as it does not attract attention away from the model itself. The figures, trees, and entourage are there to support the designer's grand creation—not overpower it.

Conclusion

Models can be made for fun, even for profit, but the general reason for making an architectural model is to sell the project behind it. To that end, the model must be accurate, appropriate, easy to understand, meticulously constructed, and well presented. Your aim is to convince the jury—i.e., the professor, the crit group, or the client—that your idea, as presented by your model, is the right one.

For the student, design idea and model work in tandem, starting out with uncomplicated projects and progressing to the more complex. From the very beginning, each model is a chance to craft something desirable. As your expertise grows, you will add more tools to your kit and more materials to your repertoire. New ideas will come from external sources. Your own creative style will begin to emerge. It is a future to look forward to.

Index